An Angel Betrayed

An Angel Betrayed

How Wealth, Power and Corruption Destroyed the JonBenet Ramsey Murder Investigation

By

David J. Hughes

Strategic Book Publishing and Rights Co.

Strategic Book Publishing and Rights Co.
12620 FM 1960, Suite A4-507
Houston TX 77065
www.sbpra.com

ISBN: 978-1-61897-708-3

Dedicated to:

My family, for loving me.

My friends, for tolerating me.

Websleuths.com, without whom none of this would be possible.

And to JonBenet, a beautiful little angel who never knew my name. I will never forget hers.

TABLE OF CONTENTS

DISCLAIMER

Unless noted, the following contains my opinions. No one has been convicted or formally charged with anything. All parties are officially innocent until proven guilty.

Introduction

The story of JonBenet Ramsey's life is one we've all seen on all those primetime cable crime shows and read in all those supermarket rag magazines: a stunningly beautiful little girl; a beauty queen at six years old. She was, as described by all who knew her, as charming, smart, and trusting.

Away from the pageant scene, JonBenet was an adorable little scamp who liked to go barefoot because she "wanted to feel the earth beneath her feet." She once asked if roses knew that their thorns hurt. She couldn't believe that anything beautiful could cause pain.

She was born on August 6, 1990. She had everything going for her: looks, money, and family.

Her father, John Bennet Ramsey, was a major executive for Access Graphics Inc., a branch of the famous Lockheed Martin aircraft company.

Her mom, Patricia Ann Paugh Ramsey, known to her many friends as Patsy, had been a beauty pageant queen from her childhood days growing up in West Virginia. JonBenet seemed to be not just following in her mother's footsteps, but outshining her.

JonBenet had an older brother named Burke, as well. He'd been so close to JonBenet since she was born, it seemed like nothing could break them up.

On the day after Christmas 1996, the world changed. JonBenet was killed, and, to this day, her killer has not been arrested.

This book seeks to answer the big questions.

WHY was JonBenet killed?

WHO killed her?

WHY haven't they been punished?

IS there any hope for this case?

This book was not written by an insider from the case. It was not written by a legal professional. It was written by a dedicated Internet crime hound who is sick and tired of year after year of injustice. It will show you how I went from being one of the biggest supporters of the Ramsey family to being one of their detractors. How the change happened to me is a story in and of itself, one you will hear and see for yourself as you continue with this book, for I intend to walk you through the evidence as I see it. I warn you: should you choose to continue, you will undoubtedly read things that will be upsetting. You will be reading the facts as I know them to be, and my opinions and speculations along the way. I think you will have moments where you will be sickened. More than likely, you will become angry. It may very well shock you. However, to stay silent is to take part in a travesty. I can stay silent no longer. You've read the stories, heard the talking heads, and watched the video.

NOW, you will hear the truth.

CHAPTER ONE

JonBenet—Little Miss Murder Victim

On the morning of December 26th, 1996, Patsy Ramsey woke up, according to her statement, at 5:22 AM. The family was scheduled to fly aboard a private airplane to Michigan to meet with members of the extended family. John Ramsey had three adult children from his first marriage. John Andrew was his son, Melinda and Elizabeth were his daughters. Sadly, Elizabeth was killed in a car wreck in 1992. Patsy Ramsey had two sisters: Pamela and Paulette, sometimes known as Polly. Her mother and father, Nedra and Donald Paugh, were in Atlanta, Georgia at the time.

The Ramsey family lived in a palatial home in Boulder, Colorado. John, originally from Michigan, was a lifelong Republican. Patsy was a Christian woman from the South. Living in a town like Boulder, home of radicals like Ward Churchill, must have been like passing into another dimension. By all those who think about such things, Boulder is often described as being permanently stuck in the late 1960s, that terrible and terribly romanticized period in time when violent crime was hip and revolutionary, war was fine as long as the "pigs" were dying, and Big Government was seen as the solution to every problem. It was a hippie commune wax museum with a pulse.

Patsy wasn't thinking about that as she descended the iron spiral staircase. She was going to brew some coffee and get everyone ready for the trip to the family summer home in Charlevoix, Michigan. From there they would head to Florida for a cruise on The Big Red Boat.

They would not make it. Patsy saw something on the stairs. It was a pad of lined note paper. Later statements would confirm that it belonged to Patsy. Printed in black ink was a letter two and one-half pages long. Here's what it said:

1. Mr. Ramsey,
2. Listen carefully! We are a
3. group of individuals that represent
4. a small foreign faction. We xx
5. respect your bussiness but not the
6. country that it serves. At this
7. time, we have your daughter in our
8. posession. She is safe and unharmed
9. and if you want her to see 1997,
10. you must follow our instructions to
11. the letter.
12. You will withdraw $118,000.00
13. from your account. $100,000 will be
14. in $100 bills and the remaining
15. $18,000 in $20 bills. Make sure
16. that you bring an adequate size
17. attaché to the bank. When you
18. get home you will put the money
19. in a brown paper bag. I will
20. call you between 8 and 10 am
21. tomorrow to instruct you on delivery.
22. The delivery will be exhausting so

23. I advise you to be rested. If
24. we monitor you getting the money
25. early we might call you early to
26. arrange an earlier delivery of the
27. money and hence a earlier
28. xxxxxxxx pick-up of your daughter.
29. Any deviation of my instructions
30. will result in the immediate
31. execution of your daughter. You
32. will also be denied her remains
33. for a proper burial. The two
34. gentlemen watching over your daughter
35. do \not/ particularly like you so I
36. advise you not to provoke them.
37. Speaking to anyone about your
38. situation, such as Police, F.B.I., etc.,
39. will result in your daughter being
40. beheaded. If we catch you talking
41. to a stray dog, she dies. If you
42. alert bank authorities, she dies.
43. If the money is in any way
44. marked or tampered with, she
45. dies. You will be scanned for
46. electronic devices and if any are
47. found, she dies. You can try to
48. deceive us, but be warned that
49. we are familiar with law enforcement
50. countermeasures and tactics. You
51. stand a 99% chance of killing
52. your daughter if you try to out
53. smart us. Follow our instructions
54. and you stand a 100% chance

55. of getting her back. You and
56. your family are under constant
57. scrutiny as well as the authorities.
58. Don't try to grow a brain
59. John. You are not the only
60. fat cat around so don't think
61. that killing will be difficult.
62. Don't underestimate us, John.
63. Use that good southern common
64. sense of yours. It is up to
65. you now John!
66. Victory !
67. S.B.T.C.

It should be noted that the xxxxxxxx indicates where the word "delivery" was crossed out. Also,I have not altered the text in any way, shape or form. I have reproduced it exactly.

Obviously, or so it seemed at the time, it was a ransom note. Statements made by John and Patsy Ramsey tell how Patsy screamed for her husband to come down. He claims he rushed downstairs from the shower that was next to their bedroom in his underwear and bathrobe. He claims he partially read it and told his wife to call 911.

Now, several things should be mentioned. The note said not to call police, but they did. Although they didn't claim to IMMEDIATELY search the house, John did claim to search the basement prior to being asked by Arndt.

Ramsey said he checked Burke's train room, where he and Fleet discussed the broken window. He then added, "I'd actually gone down there earlier that morning, and the window was broken, but I didn't see any glass around, so I assumed it was broken last summer. I used that window to get in the house one time when I didn't have a key, but the window was open, I don't know, maybe an inch, and I just kind of latched it."

What? I had to work to keep my face neutral, for while he was describing the broken window, he had also admitted going down to the basement alone and unseen before he went down with Fleet White and found the body.

I pushed on that. "Fleet had talked about earlier being down there alone and discovering that window. When you say that you found it earlier that day and latched it, at what time?"

"I don't know, probably before ten."

JonBenet: Inside the Ramsey Murder Investigation
John claims to have checked on Burke:

TT: *Right around the corner. Okay. When did you check on burke during all this? You talked about John going to check on Burke.*

PR: *Yeah. I think he ran and check on him when I was up, up there uh, you know, it just all happened so fast. I said, 'Oh, my God. What about Burke?' And I think he ran in and checked him while I was running back downstairs or something.*

TT: *Okay.*

PR: *But I remember he, you know, I think he ran and checked on him and, and he told me he was okay or whatever.*

TT: *Okay. Was Burke still in the same bed? He hadn't moved beds or anything like that?*

PR: *I don't know. I didn't go in there and look..*

Also:

LOU SMIT: *Do you remember either of you going to Burke's room at that time?*

JOHN RAMSEY: *I think we did. I think I did. I remember going to his room. I don't remember if it was directly from there to his room or if I went downstairs and back up. But we checked his room pretty shortly thereafter.*

LOU SMIT: *Was this before the police were called or after?*

JOHN RAMSEY: *I think before or at least —I'm not sure.*

LOU SMIT: *When you checked–*

JOHN RAMSEY: *Cause we called the police pretty quick.*

LOU SMIT: *Okay. When you checked his room,*

0137

what did you see and how did you–

JOHN RAMSEY: *I just looked in and he was in bed and he was asleep. I mean I knew he was there and he was okay.*

Not exactly a thorough job, was it?

Patsy dialed 911. She told the dispatcher what JonBenet looked like and that her daughter had been kidnapped. By

6:00 AM, several police officers had arrived. Before they got there, the Ramseys had already invited over several of their friends: John and Barbara Fernie, Fleet White Jr. and his wife Priscilla, JonBenet's doctor, and a family preacher, Rol Hoverstock. Little could any of the cops have imagined where this would lead. If they could have, they might have all been better off trying to herd the group out and limit the damage that had already been done to the crime scene.

Working on the assumption that this was a kidnapping, the family phone was tapped, since the note had promised to contact them that morning. Strangely, the amount of money demanded for JonBenet's safe return was $118,000. Not only was that an odd figure, since the Ramseys were millionaires who could have afforded more, but it was almost exactly the amount of John Ramsey's executive end-of-the-year bonus pay. Who would know that?

In keeping with procedure, the FBI was alerted. Ron Walker, an ace profiler, was sent over to the house. He took one look at the note and said that there hadn't been a kidnapping. The scent of deceit was beginning to circulate.

No call ever came. The house was searched, but the cops didn't find anything. Worse than that, Fleet White had been allowed to roam around the basement alone. That afternoon, slightly after 1:00 PM, Detective Linda Arndt told Fleet and John Ramsey to search the house again. It was to become the blunder to end all blunders, and set the stage for what would eventually turn a tragedy into a disgusting parody of how the American legal system envisioned by the Founding Fathers is supposed to work.

John Ramsey and Fleet White were rooting around in the basement when they came to a room that White had visited earlier. It was a small room that had a distinctive feature: a broken window. Fleet pointed it out, and John claimed he'd broken it earlier that year when he had locked himself out of the house and had never fixed it.

Finally, the two men came to a room so remote it was practically hidden. John undid a peg at the top of the door frame that acted as a latch, opened it and screamed. The light went on, and there was this mass of white material lying on the floor.

They had found John's daughter. JonBenet was clearly dead. She was discolored, and, as Arndt said, smelled of death. John grabbed her up and carried her up the stairs. White went up ahead of him, screaming for help. He later said it was odd that John had screamed *before* he had turned on the light, since the room was pitch-black and White, who had been right behind him, couldn't see into it. The sight of John carrying JonBenet in front of him was said to be a sickening sight. The little girl was in full rigor mortis with her arms over her head, rigid as a plank. He laid her on the floor of the living room.

By doing all of this, he had contaminated the body. It got worse from there, as John covered the body with a blanket right in front of the cops. Someone placed a gray Colorado Avalanche sweatshirt over the exposed feet a few minutes later. Patsy Ramsey had been sitting in a sun room directly over the site where her daughter had been laying. She'd been crying, but there were a few things that didn't add up. First, when she had answered the door to let the cops in, she had been fully made up. This woman had supposedly just woken up, put on her clothes, made up her face, went downstairs, found the note, got hysterical, called 911 in a panic, all in the space of thirty minutes. Yet, when the cops arrived, they saw a woman without a hair out of place and no tear tracks or anything like that. Moreover, one of the police officers said that when she'd been crying in the sun room, she'd had her hands over her eyes, the classic crying image. But, she'd had her fingers open and, as the officer said in his report, she'd been tracking his movements with her eyes. He wondered later if she was acting and checking to see if he was buying it.

Burke Ramsey was spared the sight of his baby sister's dead body. He had been sent to the White's house where Priscilla White and Fleet's daughter Daphne, JonBenet's friend and playmate, kept an eye on him. One has to wonder: if your daughter had just gone missing, would you let your son out of your sight for even an instant?

Patsy charged into the room and fell onto the body of JonBenet, sobbing hysterically and begging Jesus to raise her from the dead. Patsy had been diagnosed with late-stage ovarian cancer when JonBenet was about three-years-old and had undergone a painful series of treatments to beat it. During that time, she had embraced a highly evangelical form of Protestant Christianity. She was a big believer in the power of God.

At that point, instead of trying to console his wife, John Ramsey was making travel arrangements. He was attempting to fly his family out of Boulder to Atlanta, Georgia right there. That didn't happen, but it took the coroner a while to arrive, and only then did the police clear everyone out. Patsy and John didn't even ride with JonBenet's body to the morgue that evening.

CHAPTER TWO

The Investigation and The Trial That Never Was

The next morning, JonBenet's body was autopsied. When John Ramsey had found her, she'd been wrapped in a white blanket. Under that, her mouth had been covered with a piece of black duct tape. Her wrists had been tied with a white nylon cord that resembled shoelaces. Hanging from her neck was a white cord with a wooden handle. The cord had been wrapped around the wood, which was later determined to be a paintbrush belonging to Patsy Ramsey. Both ends had been broken off. The cord was then tied in a noose around the poor girl's neck and pulled so tight it crimped her neck into an hourglass shape. It got worse from there. During the examination, the coroner cut the little girl's scalp away from her skull, and the assembled police officers gaped in horror. JonBenet had also suffered a grievous head injury. It had not been visible from the outside because the skin on her head had not been broken. But on the top right of her skull was a rectangular hole half-an-inch wide where the bone had been punched out. The skull fracture continued forward, practically splitting her skull in half to the bridge of the nose.

When the coroner undressed her, he noticed two things. One, her panties were much too large on her body. Two, they had blood spots in them. So he examined her vagina. He found severe inflammation and an area of abrasion. Whoever had killed her had also violated her. But no bodily fluids like saliva or semen were found. After that, the investigation took a turn for the worse. None of the cops in Boulder had any experience with homicides. And the commander, John Eller, a macho good old boy from Florida, wasn't going to accept any help from the Denver cops, the FBI or anyone else, in a showing of extremely poor judgment. The Ramseys would not be interviewed until April of 1997, and by that time, several events had taken place.

Firstly, the District Attorney of Boulder was Alex Hunter. Hunter had been elected in the late Sixties and never voted out. And he was very much a product of the era that marked his rise. He was a defense lawyer who felt that winning wasn't everything when it came to trying criminals. And he certainly practiced what he preached. By Christmas of 1996, Alex Hunter had not taken a single case to trial in almost a decade. To say he was not an aggressive prosecutor is like saying water is wet. He spent most of his time offering plea-bargains. With such a dismal record, his thirty year tenure is hard to explain to anyone who doesn't understand the Boulder political climate, but simple once you do. Alex Hunter was a Democrat in a district where trying to get a Republican elected is like trying to empty the ocean with a spoon. There's an old saying in American politics that says you get the government you deserve. Boulder deserved Alex Hunter. In this author's humble opinion, I wouldn't trust him to prosecute a bicycle thief. He was a lousy prosecutor who had spent too many years in office, making him complacent, the same kind of complacency that allowed nineteen men on terrorist watch lists to board planes and bring down the World Trade Center towers. Upon election, he promised rehabilitation over punishment. His record speaks for itself (generously provided by JJ Maloney from crimemagazine.com):

1981: Christopher Courtney was charged with second-degree murder after Courtney shot two people dead at the Longmont Civic Center. The first trial ended in a mistrial, for reasons unknown to this author. Hunter reduced the charge to criminally negligent homicide. Courtney got away with a two-year sentence in the county jail. The mayor and city council were very displeased.

1982: Kirk Long resigned as undersheriff. In a move that almost seems like a foreshadowing of what Det. Steve Thomas would do sixteen years later, for mostly the same reasons, Long penned a letter which went public. The letter said, in part: "We in America have a legal system that is designed to be adversarial. It is apparent to me that the only adversary relationships within the legal system of the 20th Judicial District are the relationships between law enforcement agencies and the office of the District Attorney. The ignoring of compelling physical evidence, the artificial bolstering of conviction statistics through plea bargaining, deferred prosecutions, and deferred sentences speaks loudly of incompetence and political maneuvering. The essence of my belief is that the citizens of Boulder County do not have an advocate in the judicial system."

1985: It took Hunter more than two years to charge Mike Grainger with a crime, even though Grainger's obese wife was found lying in bed with a massive head wound, and there was no evidence of an intruder. Grainger got three years.

1992: The Rape Crisis Team, part of the Mental Health Center of Boulder County, penned a report, "Sexual Assault in Boulder County: The Crimes and Their Consequences." The report showed that, in 1990, of 60 cases involving children, 42 abusers avoided serving any time at all, three went to a halfway house, 13 served county jail time (half of those with work-release) and only one was sentenced to state prison.

1986: In his last major case, Hunter was named special prosecutor in neighboring Adams County to try the sheriff there, Bert Johnson. The sheriff was charged with extortion, embezzlement and sexual misconduct. Hunter offered to dismiss all charges if Johnson would resign from office, but the judge rejected the deal. Hunter lost the case at trial. He decided never to try another case.

Hunter, who did not seek re-election in 2000, made a lot of enemies over the years, but those enemies were never able to bring him down in a political sense.. Ordinarily, in a case such as JonBenet's, the danger to a prosecutor perceived as shirking his duty comes from the parents. In the through-the-looking-glass world of the Ramsey case, everything is twisted. The parents – who wield a lot of power – have showered praise on the "professionalism" of Hunter's office and scorn on the Boulder Police Department. According to Det. Thomas, Hunter and his staff are the only reason the Ramseys have avoided indictment.

Hunter's staff was a fitting compliment. In fact, the Boulder DA's office had no murder-trial experience at all—complex or otherwise—within the past five years, according to the

Denver Post. One was Peter Hofstrom, a bitchy little nudnik who thought he could identify with the police by talking about what a tough guy he was back when he was a prison guard. Another was Mary Keenan, a radical feminist just as much at home in the flower power era as Hunter, and Lawrence DeMuth III, who went by the name "Trip." He fancied himself a cowboy, and dressed to look the part. His approach toward law enforcement can be summed up in a conversation he had with Steve Thomas, one of the detectives on the case. In the first three weeks of the case, before anyone in the DA's office has seen any evidence, he'd already decided that the Ramseys would not be investigated. His reasoning was that because he had children, he couldn't imagine a parent killing their child. Thomas responded with statistics from the Justice Department showing that when a child is murdered, 11 times out of 12, it is a close family member who is responsible. Now, at first blush, it's easy to sympathize with "Trip." After all, no one wants to believe that the lady down the street could kill her own children. But as a prosecutor, he should damn well know better than that. That kind of naive thinking has no place in a DA's office. Last, and definitely least, was Bill Wise, who, for the last several years up to that point in time, had been co-owner of a building with a lawyer from the law firm of Hal Haddon, the lawyers the Ramseys hired less than a week after the killing.

Since I've mentioned them, it might be a good time to show you what the DA's office was up against. Hal Haddon's law firm was and is one of the most powerful in the entire country. Haddon, Morgan & Foreman could boast of disgraced former presidential candidate Gary Hart, Governor Roy Romer, former Governor Richard Lamm, and wackjob author Hunter S. Thompson as their past clients.

More recently, NBA star Kobe Bryant has been added to that list. They were very big in Democratic Party politics, in which Alex Hunter was involved. As Chuck Green, a reporter for the *Denver Post* put it, "Take a look at their offices here in Denver. Then take a walk over to the Governor's Mansion a few blocks away and tell me which is bigger, and I'll tell you which one is more powerful."

The DA's office might as well have tried to bring down a battleship with a BB gun.

If you research why lawyers were hired so quickly, you'll hear a different number of stories. Oddly, they're all told by the Ramseys. John claims that his friend, Michael Bynum, a lawyer himself, told him that the police had already decided that he and Patsy had done it and were trying to hang them for it. That much is consistent. The Ramseys hired some private investigators, as well. Initially, they said that they hired them to hunt down leads that the police were not running down, since they'd already decided the Ramseys were guilty. But the truth came out in a videotaped deposition in 2001, where John Ramsey admitted that he had hired the private eyes as a defense mechanism. They were hired to sabotage any future case against him and/or Patsy and, as he put it, "keep us out of jail." In that same line of questioning, he said he never even read the reports that the private investigators gave him. Sounds like John was very dedicated to finding his daughter's killer, doesn't it? Remember all of this, because I'll go into greater detail about it later.

By now it was obvious to the cops that they had a tall order to fill. But I don't think any of them imagined that the District Attorney's office would soon go from uncooperative to outright hostile. In the first few days of the case, the police wanted to keep the body of JonBenet for additional testing.

When Pete Hofstrom asked the police why the body hadn't been released yet, he became hysterical, accusing the police of attempting to "ransom" JonBenet's body in exchange for interviews with the parents. It was a ridiculous accusation. That he leaked it to the Ramseys is almost beyond belief. But, hoping to avoid a scandal, police commander John Eller released the body on the 28th. JonBenet was buried in Marietta, Georgia on New Year's Eve. The next day, John and Patsy Ramsey went on CNN, the Cable News Network, to plead for help in finding the killer.

I came across that broadcast just by chance. My heart went out to them. What they were going through was unimaginable. I was fifteen-years-old when it happened. I was a typical teenage nerd: looked at askance by many, but it didn't really bother me. For a while, I was too caught up in my own teenage crap to pursue it at any length, what with a brother in middle school who needed braces and living in a house with only our mother. My father had died of cancer in 1993. I was in a unique perspective to identify with Patsy Ramsey the more I learned about her.

What was to become interesting was that the parents were eager to talk to the media. Indeed, at times, it almost seemed like Patsy Ramsey was enjoying the attention. But they still wouldn't sit down with police, to give them what information they could while their minds were fresh. In no time at all, the case became the next OJ Simpson story, with the tabloid magazines going on a feeding frenzy. One, "The Globe," went so far as to steal and publish autopsy photos of the little girl. More and more, people saw video footage from JonBenet's pageants. The image of a baby painted up like a hooker and wearing outfits that Las Vegas showgirls would deem too skimpy would define her in the minds of the public. Some people said that the videos showed a girl who was being exploited. A few said she looked like she had been taught to move in a sexual manner to seem more poised. This was later confirmed. Months earlier, the Ramseys had hired Kit Andre, a 19-year-old dance teacher to make JonBenet more "adult." Suspicion grew about the parents.

To fight back, the Ramseys hired several public relations gurus, including one whose claim to fame was being a spin doctor for the White House during the Iran/Contra scandal.

By February, I was fully in their corner. This would change in time. After a while, it became clear that the police and the district attorney's office were not on the same page. Leaks to the tabloids from both sides were going out faster than they could be plugged up. And the assistant DAs were slow to move from their view that JonBenet was killed by an intruder. Some would not move at all. The Ramseys were making many demands of the police and DA in exchange for interviews. The DA often acquiesced, which was highly irregular. Most of the police had never seen a DA hand over so much evidence to a suspect that didn't involve discovery at trial. Search warrants were requested and denied, with the DA preferring to ask nicely. Ace profiler Gregg McCrary wondered if indictments could be brought against the DA for malfeasance.

In April, the Ramseys were interviewed for the first time. But several events were in motion. First, retired detective Andrew Louis Smit, known as Lou, had been hired by the DA's office. More on him later. Secondly, the Ramseys had hired former FBI profiler, and supposed inspiration for Thomas Harris' Hannibal Lecter books, John Douglas. More on him later as well.

More importantly, in June, the "War Room," as the police called the room where they kept the case file, had been broken into, or it appeared that way. The computers had been hacked, and evidence went MIA. Assistant district attorney Mary Keenan's pass had been used to get inside, according to the room's card scanner. The culprits were most likely in the DA's office, with "Trip" DeMuth the most likely ringleader, though nothing was ever proven. The cops no longer trusted the DA. Months went by, and as time passed, more and more people became divided into two groups. One side felt that the Ramseys were somehow involved with JonBenet's death, either having killed her or knowing who did, and those who felt that the parents were being victimized by a modern-day witch hunt and the killer was an intruder. Suspects ranged from those very well-known to the Ramseys to random skells off the street. In late 1997, the Boulder police began accepting some outside help. John Eller had left the case and new management was moving in. The Boulder Police and members of the DA's office attended a meeting with agents of CASKU. CASKU stands for Child Abduction/Serial Killer Unit. It's a unit of the FBI's Behavioral Science Unit, the profilers that determine what kind of killer a person is dealing with. In 1998, the DA, which had been equally hostile to accepting outside help, brought in Michael Kane from Pennsylvania to head up a Grand Jury if the DA decided to call one, as none of Hunter's staff had any experience with Grand Juries. Unlike the Boulder DA and his staff, Kane had a history as an aggressive, smart prosecutor who actually won tough cases. In August of 1998, Detective Steve Thomas resigned from the police force. His resignation letter to the DA was released to the press. It was a blistering condemnation of the DA's office Thomas held that the DA and his staff had sabotaged any case against the Ramseys through their incompetence. That September, Lou Smit also resigned, saying that the DA was too focused on the Ramseys. His resignation came upon Hunter's announcement that a Grand Jury would be called on the case.

In October of 1999, the Grand Jury came back, but nothing came of it. It would not be until October of 2013 that it would be revealed that the Grand Jury had voted to indict John and Patsy Ramsey, and that Alex Hunter had not gone forward with their recommendation and had misled the public.

In 2000, the Ramseys and Det. Thomas wrote books, each leading to several lawsuits. In May, the Ramseys paid for a lie detector test which they claimed to have passed. In August of that year, the Ramseys were interviewed by several members of Boulder's law enforcement establishment.

In 2001, Alex Hunter finally stepped down. Mary Keenan, who later married and changed her name to Mary Lacy, took over. Later that year, as would be repeated in Durham, NC five years later, she tried to railroad several University of Colorado, Boulder football players for a rape that never happened. In September, proceedings began in a defamation suit that would turn the case on its ear.

In August of 2002, the Boulder police publicly questioned three key pieces of the so-called "intruder theory." In reaction, the Ramseys' new lawyer, a litigation attorney from Atlanta named Leroy Lincoln Wood, Lin Wood for short, said that if the Boulder Police did not turn the case over to an entity more friendly to the intruder theory, he would sue them and obtain the case file. That December, Mary Lacy took over to placate him.

That year, a defamation lawsuit in federal court went to summary judgment. A judge, based solely on the evidence presented, said that the Ramseys were most likely innocent of the crime. The DA supported the finding. She was quickly condemned by many former case investigators for doing so. The DA then hired an entirely new investigative team completely loyal to her, purposely closing out the lawyers and advisors who had worked the case for six years, much the way Joseph Stalin eliminated his "enemies."

In 2004, John Ramsey ran for state senate in Michigan on the Republican ticket, claiming that George W. Bush was a great inspiration to him. He was soundly defeated.

In June of 2006, Patsy Ramsey died when her cancer came back with a vengeance. She was only 49-years-old. It was my dad's birthday. He would have been 61.

In August of 2006, John Mark Karr, a former schoolteacher and known pedophile was arrested in Thailand. He had confessed to a University of Colorado professor that he had killed the little beauty. The DA dragged him back to the United States to investigate, with most newspapers announcing that the killer had finally been found. But practically before Karr was back on American soil, his story began to unravel, and the DA's case against him with it. After a two-week frenzy, the DA announced that Karr was nothing but a crank who had been trying for several years to insert himself into the case. Mary Lacy was roundly condemned for her hasty actions, with some claiming she was doing it to prevent the case from being taken from her hands. Others went so far as to claim that she was in the tank for the Ramseys.

On July 9th, 2008, outgoing DA Mary Lacy announced that she had cleared the Ramsey family of any suspicion. Her decision was based on the findings of a new, controversial

DNA testing method. Nothing ever came of it, and on January 13, 2009. Lacy stepped down for good and was replaced with Stan Garnett.

On February 2, 2009, Garnett and Chief Mark Beckner announced that the Boulder Police Department would re-assume command of the case, forming a special unit including agents from the FBI, the Colorado Bureau of Investigation, the Denver Police Department, and several other local agencies. They announced that they would handle it as a "cold case."

As you will see in the following chapters, this case is anything but cold. As those who were associated with the case can tell you, it's not just hot, it's radioactive, contaminating everyone and everything that comes into contact with it. Just ask James Kolar, a former member of Mary Lacy's team who broke his silence in 2012 with a book that is extremely critical of the intruder theory. Until then, the journey begins here.

CHAPTER THREE

JonBenet-Loved To Death

This is where it gets ugly.

I believe that Patsy Ramsey killed her daughter and then she and John Ramsey tried to cover it up. I realize that is a horrible thought. How I came to believe it, when I was so deeply in their corner, is a bizarre story. Here is what I think happened. The Ramseys had attended a party on Christmas night at the house of Fleet and Priscilla White. When they got home, both parents said that they put JonBenet to bed and John worked with Burke on a model train set for a while. After that, it becomes a nightmare: The Ramseys get home from the party at the Whites'. Burke asks for a bedtime snack. Patsy sees a bowl of pineapple on the kitchen counter and gives him some, telling him not to paw at it. Both children have some.

JOHN: "Come on, honey. Let's get you to bed. Be with you in a minute, son."

BURKE: "I'll wait for you there, Dad."

PATSY: "Just a quick check to see if I missed anything."

Patsy is now alone. She's doing her thing. John puts JonBenet in bed. They speak for a minute. Maybe something else. Maybe he gives her privates a "quick check." He goes down to the basement.

Patsy's catching her breath in the living room. John and Burke come up.

JOHN: Head on up to bed, son.

BURKE: "Okay, Dad."

The parents are alone.

JOHN: "Come on up to bed."

PATSY: "No, I'm not done yet."

JOHN: "You shouldn't take so much on yourself."

PATSY (irritated at him): "I have to. I do everything around here."

JOHN: "Sorry I mentioned it."

John goes upstairs. Soon, JonBenet is back down.

PATSY: "What do you want now, honey," with a little irritation in her voice.

JONBENET: "I did it again."

PATSY: "Oh, God. Come on."

Up to JonBenet's room.

PATSY: "I don't see anything."

JONBENET: "I didn't go to bed yet."

PATSY: "Can't you do anything I ask?"

JONBENET: "I'm sorry."

PATSY: "Get in there."

Into the bathroom. Patsy cleans her up.

PATSY: "Here, don't tell your father."

JONBENET: "You and Daddy tell me secrets."

PATSY: "Secrets?"

JONBENET: "Yeah, Daddy tells me to keep secrets."

PATSY: "Like what?"

JONBENET (suddenly sullen): "It wouldn't be a secret then."

PATSY (now more irritated): "Fine."
Patsy becomes rough.

JONBENET: "OW! Mommy, that hurts! Daddy's nicer."

PATSY: "I didn't think your father cleaned you up."

JONBENET: "He doesn't. He calls it our special game."

PATSY's head snaps up. Their eyes meet.

JONBENET (whispering): "I told the secret."

PATSY (in a rage): "YOU ROTTEN LITTLE LIAR!!!"

JONBENET (almost in a panic): "I'm sorry, Mommy!"

PATSY: "I'll teach you a lesson you won't forget!"

JonBenet tries to run away, but her pants are still around her knees. She tries to pull them up, but trips. As she gets up, Patsy grabs her collar and begins to struggle with her. She MEANS to toss JonBenet onto the bed face-first and spank the daylights out of her. But during the fight, JonBenet takes a hard blow that cracks her skull.

Patsy sees JonBenet crumpled on the floor.

PATSY: "That won't work, you little faker. You're in big trouble."

She picks JonBenet up and lays her on the bed. But she's so limp.

PATSY: "I said, cut it out."

Nothing. JonBenet is in shock and doesn't seem to be breathing.

PATSY (anger replaced by worry): "JonBenet Patricia Ramsey, you cut that out right now. Baby? (Now panicked): BABY?! PLEASE say something! Oh, GOD, I didn't mean to! No, oh, God, no! Not my baby!"

John comes in.

JOHN: "What the hell is going on in here?!"

Patsy turns. Her eyes are full of tears and hate. She blitzes him.

PATSY: "YOU BASTARD!"

He grabs her wrists. "Are you crazy?!" He sees JonBenet. "What did you do?!"

PATSY: "Me?! You couldn't get it from me, so you took her! And I believed YOU!"

JOHN: "You stupid, crazy bitch! I have to save her!"

PATSY: "It's too late now! She's dead!"

JOHN: "NO! That's impossible!" (Keep in mind, John's lost Beth.)

PATSY: "I'll see you rot for this!"

JOHN: "How?! You killed her."

Patsy fights until she's fought-out. She collapses to the floor, sobbing.

JOHN: "Honey..."

PATSY: "We can't leave her like this. She's so beautiful. like an angel. She deserves better."

JOHN: "I can't believe this. Burke...what will happen to him?"

PATSY: "He can't ever know about this. He can't think we killed JonBenet."

JOHN: "How do we make this right?"

PATSY: "I thought you were the big expert!"

JOHN: "Shut up! I'm trying to think."

PATSY: "What kind of person would do this?"

JOHN: "The kind we saw in the Navy. Damn, I wish I could remember who they were."

And it just spirals from there. Putting anything they can think of into a possible scenario, they stage a scene. But Patsy's dramatic flair puts it over the top. John, wracked with guilt, knows she hangs by a hair, so he says nothing. He also knows that the truth will put them in prison where the inmates will do horrible things to them...

PATSY: "What kind of knot do we use?"

JOHN: "Do it yourself."

Patsy ties a sloppy noose and sloppier wrist ties.

JOHN: "I can't even look at her like that."

They think about bundling her up to dump, but it's too risky. In the basement.

PATSY: "Wouldn't she have been messed with down there?"

JOHN: "Don't ask me to–"

PATSY: "You already DID! That's how we got into this mess."

JOHN: "I can't touch her like this." He uses the brush to avoid touching her privates. His fibers end up on her, having scuffed off his sleeve on her clothing when he pulls his arm back. "Can you write left-handed?"

PATSY: "Yeah, but–"

JOHN: "Come on."

John dictates part of the note, she writes. At this point, she's caught up in this. Her greatest pageant, her greatest adventure. It's exhilarating.

In short, Patsy Ramsey heard her daughter say that John had been molesting her. Her general state of over tiredness combined with shock and disbelief which turned to anger, in my opinion. It's a sad fact that many mothers, upon being told by their child that their spouse is a molester, tend to deny it vehemently, not wanting to face the awful possibility. Worse than that, they tend to blame the victim. Marilyn Van Derbur Atler is a former Miss America who was molested as a child by her father. When she told her mother about it, she was not believed and was punished for telling such filthy lies. Clearly, Patsy did not mean to kill her darling daughter. It just happened and she didn't see a way out. After that, in my opinion, Patsy's natural inclination towards the flashy and overdone took over and she decided to give her daughter a death that was as spectacular as her life. It just wouldn't do to have a child beauty queen with such a bright future taken in such a mundane way. But if it could look like JonBenet had been killed in her own home by a popular bogeyman, the kind who gets people thinking with their emotions rather than their good sense, right under the noses of her parents, that would be a fitting death. I'm merely speculating, but I think Patsy figured that JonBenet would make her famous as a beauty queen. With JonBenet dead, that was no longer an option. But make a good crime scene and do your best acting job and you will become a magnet for sympathy. And being a suspect makes you that much more sympathetic. Here's what I mean: Patsy was writing the story of her lifetime, with herself as the hero. And the hero of a story is only as good as the villain is evil. Patsy's story had two villains. One was the intruder she created who took her daughter, the second was the police force which, to hear her tell it, was out to fry her in the electric chair. She becomes the ultimate victim. Michael Kane did an interview in 2002 where he said that the staging of the crime was so overdone, it would have to have been done by someone with a proclivity for showmanship. He used these words: "It was a very theatrical production and Patsy is a very theatrical person." He described her as a narcissist who "loves being known as the mother of a murdered beauty queen." It's an old story. History is full of people who, once they've outlived their usefulness, have become worth more to a cause dead than alive. Che Guevara is a good example, as is John F. Kennedy. Or the one that JonBenet seemed destined to accompany, Marilyn Monroe. Let me lay this illustration on you. Patsy often likened her daughter to Marilyn Monroe, even printing it on JonBenet's name badge at one pageant. Who better to associate your beauty queen daughter with than the most famous blonde of all time? But, what most people overlook is this: one of the big reasons why Marilyn's legend is so strong is because she died tragically. Marilyn died young and at the peak of her fame, her beauty undiminished. She was not allowed to grow old and obscure. Well, what happened to Marilyn happened to JonBenet, and I can't help but wonder if for the same reason. I don't necessarily mean that JonBenet's death was premeditated (although, there may be those who do). I'm just saying that, if it did start out as an unintentional killing, it might explain to all those naysayers why 911 wasn't called and why all of the staging was done: a child beauty queen, so destined for greatness killed in a common, garden-variety, run-of-the-mill, humdrum domestic incident? That would NEVER do! She was so spectacular in life. She HAD to be spectacular in death. Nothing but the best (or worst, depending on how you see it) for JonBenet. And she IS spectacular in death! Her death made her more well-known to more people than all of her performances put together. Not to mention that it's almost 20 years later and people STILL remember her! I admit, I'm just speculating, but in good faith, based on the opinions of people like Mike Kane and Patsy's own behavior, namely putting such a profound, almost obsessive investment in her daughter and likening her to beautiful blondes who died tragically, such as Marilyn Monroe. This whole thing SCREAMS "drama queen." It didn't stop there. When Diana Spencer, Princess of Wales, known to many as Princess Di, was killed in a car accident in France, Patsy did her best to capture a little spotlight from that tragedy as well, saying that JonBenet was "America's Princess Diana." Like Marilyn herself, Diana was known for her stunning beauty. Fate had played a cruel trick on Diana as well, and she too would not be allowed to grow old and obscure.

I appreciate how terrible it must have been to read that. Here's how I got there. The police amassed an extensive case file. I present only a small sample here:

1) Fibers from the sweater Patsy Ramsey was known to have worn that night were found on the sticky side of the duct tape over JonBenet's mouth. Several people have tried to claim that this proves nothing because the tape had been removed from JonBenet's mouth by her father and handled by others, thus they could have transferred innocently. But those same fibers were found inside the blanket that JonBenet was wrapped up in, and were found inside the little box that Patsy Ramsey kept her art supplies in. Remember, one of her brushes had formed the handle of the ligature that JonBenet was strangled with. But most notably, those fibers were found tied into the knots of the cord itself. No such fibers were found directly on JonBenet's body, which almost eliminates the possibility of an innocent transfer. Here is an excerpt from an interview Patsy and Lin Wood conducted with three representatives from the Boulder DA's office in August of 2000. Michael Kane, Bruce Levin, and Mitch Morrissey were the representatives.

Q. Frequently would be three or four times —I mean, was it, if you are chilly, was this the item that you always threw on? That is what I am getting at.

A. *Not necessarily, no.*

Q. *You talked about, in your '98 interview, that you, on the 24th, that you were in the basement and you were wrapping presents. Do you know, when you were doing that, whether or not you had on that coat?*

A. *I don't know.*

Q. *You have told us that you painted as a hobby. Would you wear this coat to paint?*

A. *No.*

Patsy established that she didn't wear that sweater down to the basement.

MR. LEVIN: *I can state to you, Mr. Wood, that, given the current state of the scientific examination of fibers, that, based on the state of the art technology, that I believe, based on testing, that fibers from your client's coat are in the paint tray.*

MR. WOOD: *Are you stating as a fact that they are from the coat or is it consistent with? What is the test result terminology? Is it conclusive? I mean, I think she is entitled to know that when you ask her to explain something.*

MR. KANE: *It is identical in all scientific respects.*

MR. WOOD: *What does that mean? Are you telling me it is conclusive?*

MR. KANE: *It is identical.*

MR. WOOD: *Are you saying it is a conclusive match?*

MR. KANE: *You can draw your own conclusions.*

MR. WOOD: *I am not going to draw my own conclusions.*

MR. KANE: *I am saying it is identical.*

MR. WOOD: *Well, what you are saying in terms of how you interpret a lab result may or may not be the lab result. If you have it, let's see it. I would be glad to let her answer a question about it, but I don't want to go into the area of where we are dealing with someone's interpretation of something that may not be a fact and have her explain something because she can't explain something that might be someone's opinion or someone's interpretation. She can try to answer something if you are stating it as a matter of fact.*

MR. LEVIN: *Well, I believe that Mr. Kane's statement is accurate as to what the examiner would testify to.*

MR. WOOD: *Will he testify that it is a conclusive match?*

MR. KANE: *Yes.*

Perhaps Mr. Kane can be forgiven a slight overstatement. Fibers cannot truly be called "identical." The forensic testing as stands now isn't that advanced. The term is "consistent with," but that's just legalese. If someone says your fibers are consistent with something, you're pretty much screwed. Fiber analysis does not just involve matching the color. The first step is to compare fibers from various clothing items to the fibers found at the scene. This is done through a microscope. During this process, the fibers in question will be examined to see how well they match up in various ways. For example, if a fiber is described as "red," it will be unraveled to see if any other threads are mixed in with the red threads in order to produce a different shade. White threads may be interwoven to get a lighter red. Black threads may be interwoven to get a darker red. After that, the fibers will be tested for chemical treatments. This helps determine what chemicals, if any, were used to make the item and what it is made of. It could be acrylic, wool, cotton, velvet, polyester, satin, silk, or any of various fabrics. Once that match has been made, the manufacturer will be contacted. They should be able to tell the investigator where and when the item was made and who it is generally sold by, such as Bloomingdales, Sears, and so on. Once that has been accomplished, the seller may be able to tell how many were sold. That allows the police to track the owner. In this case, it was Patsy Ramsey.

Q. *(By Mr. Levin) Mrs. Ramsey, I have scientific evidence from forensic scientists that say that there's fibers in the paint tray that match your red jacket. I have no evidence from any scientist to suggest that those fibers are from any source other than your red jacket.*

Bruce Levin made this statement on the record. On the videotape of this interview, Patsy Ramsey, upon hearing what Levin has just said, changes her demeanor. She goes from calm and composed to severely rattled. Her head droops, her mouth contorts into a sickly smile, and she looks as though she might faint. I wonder why she acted like that if she were innocent. What's more, she made no attempt to answer the question and give a possible innocent explanation. Two years later, she told a CBS reporter that her fibers had transferred to JonBenet that morning because Patsy, who had been wearing the same clothing she had worn at the party, laid on top of her. But this cannot explain it. In their own book, *Death of Innocence,* John Ramsey writes that by the time Patsy came near the body, JonBenet was already fully covered. This is borne out by the police reports. Oh, dear. Patsy made a boo-boo. She might have wanted to ask her lawyer for her money back if she gave him any. Even if it were true, since it was clearly an attempt to hoodwink people, the fibers would have to have floated down the stairs into the basement around several corners to reach the blanket that JonBenet had been wrapped in. As Boston sex crimes prosecutor Wendy Murphy stated, this would require, quote, "flat-out magic." Moreover, the blanket was fresh from the dryer and Patsy's sweater had not been laundered with it. Her own story does not hold up. Think about that: this woman had two full years to come up with a story, and that was the best she could do.

2) Patsy claimed that she saw the ransom letter on the spiral staircase and stepped over it before turning to see what it was. The police later conducted an experiment where they tried to recreate her story. None of the police officers could do it without falling. Again, her story makes no sense.
3) Patsy Ramsey claimed that she had never seen the cord or the tape that JonBenet was bound up with. And it is true that no cord or tape roll were ever found in the house. But it is not quite as simple as all that. The police found out that both the cord and tape were sold at a local hardware store. It was named McGuckin's Hardware. So the police checked out the store. The store's receipts did not list the items bought, only the prices of the items bought. But that was a start. So the police went over Patsy Ramsey's credit card records. The records said that she had made some purchases from McGuckin's in the weeks leading up to the killing. The prices on the items matched the prices of the tape and the cord. Sadly, the records probably cannot be used in court because they were obtained illegally. The police did not obtain them illegally, but they were stolen by a group that gathers information on the rich and well-connected and then sells it as blackmail information to the highest bidder. They called themselves "Dirty Deeds Done Dirt Cheap," and this information was made public through a Congressional hearing in 1997 after the "Dirty Deeds" director was sent to prison on a RICO charge for his activities. All told, it's

not a lead-pipe cinch by a long shot, but I don't believe in coincidences.

4) Though I do not speak from personal experience on how one "should" behave upon finding one's child killed, Patsy and John have behaved oddly, to say the least. In 2000, she practically dared the police and prosecutors to put her on trial, saying, quote, "If you think I did it, let's have a trial and get it over with." I can't think of a more blatant attempt to stick a thumb in the eye of law enforcement. She was telling them, "Fuck you. I'm right here, I'm not giving up shit, and you'll never prove I did it because I'm too smart, too rich and too pretty." When it looked like a grand jury would indict her, she wondered if prison stripes "would make me look fat," and wondered if she could bring her red velvet pillow along. I did not find out about these little musings of hers until several years afterwards, and by then it made me angry. Her kid's been murdered right under her nose, and she thinks it's all a big game!

   It doesn't help that she and her husband seem to have an ego problem, to say the least. When I watch someone like Mark Lunsford, Brenda Van Dam, and especially Marc Klaas, they always speak about the horrific things done to their children and the pain and terror they must have been in during those horrible last moments. Not the Ramseys. No, sir. The only pain they talk about is their own! How DARE the police treat them like suspects. Me, Me, Me, Me!

That's all I ever hear from them! Their own book, *Death of Innocence* is full of that kind of garbage, about how they've been victimized twice: first by the killer, then by the cops. During their New Years Day 1997 CNN appearance, Patsy Ramsey said that JonBenet was better off dead because JonBenet would never have to experience the pain of cancer or the pain of losing a child. In other words, instead of trying to put herself in the shoes of her daughter and feel her pain, she was thankful that JonBenet would never feel her pain or John's pain, by extension suggesting that JonBenet's pain was less important. John Ramsey talks about how he regrets that the FBI wasn't called in immediately (which is a lie, since Ron Walker was there that morning), but when the offer was made to the Ramseys to have the FBI take over the case, he said no. He said that the FBI was tainted because they had worked with the Boulder Police and were somehow part of this giant conspiracy to "get" him and Patsy. Sure, like the FBI doesn't have anything better to do than put the frame on wealthy, white people in this country! Tell me another one, Johnny. I can see your nose growing from here. As Det. Thomas asked him, "who do you want to investigate this case, the Border Patrol?" Sometimes I think that John and Patsy, both of whom were familiar with the OJ Simpson trial, were using the same tactic that kept the "Juice" out of prison: when all else fails, put the police on trial. With the five-star legal talent John's wealth was able to amass, it was like shooting a hornet with an elephant gun. Some people, they know who they are, will believe anything bad about cops. All the Ramseys would need is one person like that on a jury. Too bad they didn't put them on trial just after the September 11th attacks, when we all saw the tape of New York City Policemen rushing into the burning towers to save people trapped in there. Maybe they haven't heard: cops are heroes now.

Probably the lowest point came in 2000 when the Ramseys announced that they were starting a foundation dedicated to helping children. Not just the ones victimized by violence, but children whose parents wished for them to have a "proper spiritual upbringing." They called it the SHOES Foundation. They were probably inspired by Lou Smit's favorite saying, "Who will stand in the victim's shoes?" Not only did it not pull in anywhere near the level of money it would have needed just to stay in operation, but according to the Internal Revenue Service documents, cheerfully provided us by www.thesmokinggun.com, the Ramseys themselves contributed almost none of their own money to it. Worst of all, they used the proceeds from their book, in which they promised all proceeds would go toward the foundation, to fund more of their legal defense and public relations functions, much of which took the form of a flyer campaign maligning the police. How low can you get?

5) Burke Ramsey mentioned that whoever killed JonBenet took out a knife. At the time, that was not a publicly released fact. But a knife was involved. Burke Ramsey had a Swiss army knife, but he had a habit of whittling with it inside the house and leaving wood shavings all over, so Linda Hoffmann-Pugh, the family housekeeper, took it away from him and put in a cabinet in the basement where he couldn't get to it. Only Burke, Linda Hoffmann-Pugh, and Patsy knew where it was. The knife was not used as a weapon on JonBenet, but it was found near her body.
6) Earlier, I mentioned that the police were being advised by the FBI CASKU division. Other profilers who worked the case included Ron Walker, Gregg McCrary, Roger DePue, Robert Ressler and Clint Van Zandt. Let's take a look at what they had to say about the crime.

    Two books were written about the case within a few months of each other. One was Lawrence Schiller's *Perfect Murder, Perfect Town*. The other one was *JonBenet: Inside the Ramsey Murder Investigation*, by Boulder Detective Steve Thomas. Each one spoke at length about the FBI meeting in Quantico, Virginia. As Thomas recounts in his book, over 20 CASKU team members, including hair and fiber experts, attended the August 1997 meeting. CASKU agents reported that of the more than 1,700 murdered children they had studied since the 1960s, there was only one case in which the victim was a female under the age of 12, who had been murdered in her home by strangulation, with sexual assault and a ransom note present: JonBenet Ramsey. Thomas wrote that the FBI team said the crime "did not fit an act of sex or revenge or one in which money was the motivation. Taken alone, they said, each piece of evidence might be argued, but together, enough pebbles become a block of evidentiary granite." Thomas reported that "CASKU observed that they had never seen anything like the Ramsey ransom note. Kidnapping demands are usually terse, such as 'We have your kid. A million dollars. Will call you.' From a kidnapper's point of view, the fewer words, the less police have to go on." The FBI, according to Thomas, "believed that the note was written in the house, after the murder, and indicated panic. Ransom notes are normally written prior to the crime, usually proofread, and not written by hand, in order to disguise the authorship." Thomas said the FBI deemed the entire crime "criminally unsophisticated," citing the child being left on the premises, the oddness of the $118,000 demand in relation to the multi-million dollar net worth of the Ramseys, and the concept of a ransom delivery where one would be "scanned for electronic devices." Kidnappers prefer isolated drops for the ransom delivery, not wanting to chance a face-to-face meeting. CASKU profilers also observed that placing JonBenet's body in the basement indicated the involvement of a parent, rather than an intruder. A parent would not want to place the body outside in the frigid night. They pointed out the use of the blanket that was found on her that day. It's been characterized as just having been thrown over her, but in his 1998 interview, John said that whoever did it had taken enough time to carefully tuck her in, like a "papoose."

MIKE KANE: *This is really important. That blanket, I mean, was it like there was care taken? It was neatly folded?*

JOHN RAMSEY: *I thought so, yeah.*

MIKE KANE: *It wasn't like it was just barely thrown over her?*

JOHN RAMSEY: *No, it looked like somebody was trying to make her comfortable, because it was under her, completely under her head and brought up around her, as if you would wrap a–*

MIKE KANE: *Papoose?*

JOHN RAMSEY: *–a papoose.*

It's likely the blanket was pulled fresh out of the dryer. What intruder would go rooting through the clothes? Even more importantly, inside the blanket with JonBenet was a pink nightgown with the popular doll Barbie on it. JonBenet's grandmother said it was JonBenet's favorite article of clothing, and that she treated it like a security blanket, even when she wasn't wearing it. She'd even rub it on her face to feel better. That seems like an awful lot of care and trouble for an intruder, does it not?

The CASKU professionals also stated, according to Thomas, that the ligatures "indicated staging rather than control, and the garrote was used from behind so the killer could avoid eye contact, typical of someone who cares for the victim." Thomas said the profilers had the gut feeling that "no one intended to kill the child." This would mean that the severe blow to the head was done in a thoughtless rage and that all the subsequent assault on JonBenet and the writing of the ransom note was staged to cover up the unintentional murder.

In *Perfect Murder, Perfect Town*, Schiller contends that the CASKU profilers said that the ransom note was "staging within staging." This means that, having created a phony crime, the perp needed to create a criminal. Though I personally do not speak from any specialized experience, I have studied enough true crime to make a few educated observations. Firstly, the ransom note is full of conflicting motives. While the child's body was done up to suggest a sadistic-control pedophile, the ransom note contains elements of ransom kidnappers, extreme leftist revolutionaries and Islamic radicals. These are all popular bogeymen, the kind that cause people to take leave of their senses. While the odds of actually being victimized by any of these forces is very low, the media makes them seem to be around every corner, especially when spurred on by opportunistic politicians. In turn, people will often rely more on their emotions than their good sense and take great measures to protect themselves. Let's face it, if people were not afraid of pedophiles and the idea of random kidnappings, television programs like *Law & Order: Special Victims Unit* and *To Catch a Predator* would not be as popular as they are. The problem is, around 2002, American television screens were absolutely inundated with stories of little girls kidnapped, raped and murdered. And not one of them even remotely resembles what happened to JonBenet. As for Islamic terrorism, the note does not state it specifically (there's no mention of Allah, for instance) but seems to imply it through the use of "foreign faction" and "beheading." Even before September 11, 2001 it was common knowledge among middle Americans that they chop off heads in the Middle East. Not only that, but the year JonBenet was killed, 1996 was, in retrospect, a milestone, because it was the first time that American television screens broadcast the face and the name of Osama bin Laden, the head of the Al-Qaeda network that perpetrated the 9/11 attacks. Up until then, his name was only known to CIA agents and politicians. I think it's helpful to remember that John Ramsey is a Navy man. He was stationed in the Philippines during the 1980s, right around the time of the uprising against the dictator Ferdinand Marcos. A lot of radical elements fought the Marcos regime and the democratic governments that have followed. Some are communist, like the New People's Army. Others are Islamist, such as Abu Sayyef. I wonder if these events were in the minds of the Ramsey parents and they just couldn't spell Hizbollah or Jihad or Jemaat-i-Islamiyah. After all, not even the government can agree on how to spell those names half the time.

In short, the note seems to be an attempt to play on popular fears, much the way Susan Smith tried to play on popular fears of young black men in the South when she described the man who supposedly carjacked her and took off with her sons as little more than a racist caricature of a jive-talking gangsta. Patsy Ramsey, during the New Year's Day CNN plea, tried to play on those same fears when she told all mothers across America to "hold your babies close. There's a killer out there."

It doesn't help that the paper belonged to Patsy, as did the Sharpie felt pen used to write it. The writer even put it back in the cup that held it when they finished.

7) The ransom note is not the end of the staging of this scene. The body itself. The autopsy report noted that JonBenet's wrists were tied with the same kind of cord that the ligature was made out of. It lists the length of cord between each wrist as 15-1/2 inches long. That's over a foot of space. Her arms were not tied together. They weren't tied behind her. The extra length wasn't

attached to anything. There was over a foot of space between her arms! You're telling me that would have restrained her? Not only that, the cuffs on her wrists were so loose that they left no marks. One of them slipped right off of her arm when John Ramsey carried her up the stairs.

8) As I mentioned earlier, JonBenet had tape on her mouth when she was found. I guess this was supposed to give the impression that she had been gagged, but again, whoever did it did a lousy job. For one thing, it was not tied around her head. It wasn't even a long strip. It was a small square of tape. Thomas, in his book, describes what the forensic technicians found on the tape. They discovered that it contained a perfect print of JonBenet's lips. She had not made any attempt to fight against it. It also had bloody mucous from JonBenet's nose under it. The logical conclusion, and the one that the police drew, was that it had been put on after JonBenet was dead. Why would a kidnapper put tape on someone's mouth? Easy: to keep them quiet. But this one didn't bother until after she was dead. Why? To make it look like a kidnapping gone bad.

9) As I may have mentioned previously, when Patsy Ramsey greeted police on the morning after Christmas, she had on the same red sweater and black pants that she had worn to the party the night before. Her explanation has always been that since she wore them for only a short time, they were perfectly good to wear again. This does

not jibe with what others have claimed. The family housekeeper, Linda Hoffmann-Pugh, has claimed that the idea of wearing the same clothes twice in a row was repellent to Patsy. I mean, she had a full closet full of fancy-schmancy clothes and was described by her stepson, John Andrew Ramsey, as "flashy." She doesn't seem like she'd make a habit out of doing it. Apparently, word reached her ears that the police were looking askance at this little fact, because she showed up to an interview wearing the same outfit she'd worn at a television appearance the day before. I forget specifically when this was, but Det. Thomas describes it in his own book. How did Patsy catch onto this? More on that later. But her wearing the same clothes might not mean anything to the case one way or another except that, per my pet theory, she never went to sleep that night. *Denver Post* columnist Chuck Green wrote in December of 2006 that the investigators, having inspected her bedroom, felt "that her side of the Ramsey bed hadn't been slept in."

Speaking of which, there is a photo of JonBenet's bed taken on Dec. 26th, 1996. It barely looks to have been used. If any of you reading this have children, did any of them ever leave the bed that neat when they were six-years-old? I sure didn't!

10) I mentioned that Patsy, in my vision, had told her son Burke not to grab the dish of pineapple. I say that because he must have. His fingerprints were found on the bowl, as were Patsy's own. But

none were from JonBenet. She could not have reached that bowl on the kitchen counter, per Patsy's own statements. Someone had to get the pineapple for her. We will revisit the pineapple issue later on.

11) The cord around JonBenet's neck had a fair amount of slack in it between where it was tied to the cord and where it met her neck. To use it effectively, the person would have to pull the cord up over their head almost; or wrap it around their arm. Not a very practical job, on the whole. The autopsy photos present a grim and grisly image of JonBenet's neck squeezed into an hourglass from the strangulation. To the eye, it looks horrific. Indeed, this has led many people to believe that no parent could do this to their child. But the autopsy reveals that there were no marks on JonBenet's tongue or on the inside of her mouth that would indicate her to have fought her killer. The report also reveals that the larynx, the strap muscles of the neck and the hyoid bone were all undamaged. In 1999, former Denver DA Norm Early was reported to have stated that when you stage strangulation, "you don't want the coroner to come back and say, 'oh, this couldn't have really killed somebody.' So you pull it deeper and deeper." Also, the little girl's hair was tied into both the neck knot and the handle knot. This means that the garrote was made on her body, not prepared ahead of time.

12) There is disagreement over whether or not JonBenet's skull fracture was caused by striking an

object or by being struck. Many of the detectives think she could have been thrown or slammed into a hard, curved surface such as a bathtub edge, bedpost or other such emplacement. But Dr. Werner Spitz did an experiment. He took a super-tough Maglite flashlight coated with rubber and smashed the test skull of a six-year-old child. It produced a wound almost identical to JonBenet's. Spitz claimed that the end with the lens and bulb fit the fracture perfectly. It just so happens that the Ramseys had a super-tough, rubber-coated Maglite flashlight. No fingerprints were found on it or inside it. Even the batteries were wiped clean. Why?

13) Now we'll take a look at what some of the other profilers had to say.

Roger L. DePue is a former head of the FBI Behavioral Sciences Unit. In 2006, he told reporter Ronald Kessler that Patsy Ramsey fit the profile of the person who wrote the ransom note. Apparently, he was making public what he and psychiatrist Dr. Bertram Brown had told Alex Hunter in the early days of the case. Depue, who wrote "Between Good and Evil: A Master Profiler's Hunt for Society's Most Violent Predators" with Susan Schindehette, said that on its face, the kidnap note makes no sense. "It demands a ransom for the return of JonBenet, but she was already dead," Depue said. "Since her body was in the house, a kidnapper would have had to realize that she would be found before any ransom was paid.

The note appears to be an effort to obfuscate why she died." The fact that the note was two and a half pages long "suggests that the killer was not hurrying out of fear of being caught, as one might expect," Depue said. "To kill a child and then write a note of that length suggests that either the killer was so bold that he was mentally deranged or that he was a member of the family and had no reason to be concerned. The killer even had the time to start a previous draft and discard it." The note's demand that the Ramseys withdraw $118,000.00 from their account is significant, Depue said. That amount was John Ramsey's bonus that year. "The use of the figure shows that the writer knew Ramsey and his finances," Depue said. "Moreover, the sum is ridiculously low. Given John Ramsey's wealth, a legitimate kidnapper would have demanded at least $1 million for the return of his daughter. Even more interesting, the demand that John withdraw the money from his account suggests that the writer knew that he had that much money in a single account. Perhaps the bonus had just been deposited and not yet disbursed to investment accounts." "The delivery will be exhausting so I advise you to be rested," the note says. Depue called that an unusual instruction. "The statement sounds caring, motherly," he said. "That fits in with the relatively small amount of money demanded. The writer only wants John Ramsey's bonus, something he can part with easily. Interestingly, at this point the writer switches to the pronoun 'I.' The pretext of a group demanding money has been dropped." The note warns that if the instructions are not carried out precisely, "You will also be denied her remains for proper burial." Depue said. "In my opinion, proper burial is of more concern to a female than to a male," Depue said. "The two gentlemen watching over your daughter do not particularly like you so I advise you not to provoke them," the note says. The idea of "gentlemen watching over" has a feminine tone, Depue said. "Watching over" is also a caring concept, he said. "Follow our instructions and you stand a 100 percent chance of getting her back," the note said. "You and your family are under constant scrtiny [sic] as well as the authorities. Don't try to grow a brain John." The phrase "don't try to grow a brain John" is familiar usage that "makes it clear that the writer knows John Ramsey intimately enough to chide him," Depue said. "Don't underestimate us, John," the note says. "Use that good Southern common sense of yours." That phrase is complimentary and suggests the writer is from the south, Depue said. Patsy Ramsey was born in West Virginia. So, Depue said, "The writer knows he is from the south and again refers to him as 'John.' This person knows John pretty damn well." In Depue's opinion, "The writer is a well-educated, middle-aged female. The writer used the term 'fat cat,' suggesting that the person is middle aged. 'Fat cat' is a term used in

> the 1960s and 1970s. The writer," Depue said, "is a close relative, friend, or business associate, in that order." Depue said that conclusion and the circumstances surrounding the note fit the profile of Patricia Ramsey.

During the brief media frenzy in the summer of 2006, former FBI profiler Clint Van Zandt was interviewed several times over a period of days. During an interview with cable news outlet MSNBC, Van Zandt said that he and several other profilers had studied the note and concluded that the writer was either a woman or a "very genteel male." He listed ten points of interest. Here are a few of them:

1–Claiming to be part of a terrorist organization is a common ruse in ransom notes. Van Zandt says he sees 'no linguistic evidence' to imply a foreign connection.

5–Despite threats of violence throughout the note, Van Zandt says, it has a 'softness' suggesting its author was a woman or perhaps a 'genteel man.'

6–The letter is full of commanding phrases like this one about 'immediate execution.' To Van Zandt, they point to an author used to exerting authority over others.

7–The line 'If we catch you talking to a stray dog, she dies' echoes the movie 'Dirty Harry,' as do other phrases. Van Zandt says: 'This is a novice trying to sound like an experienced criminal.'

8–The note's salutation is formal, but here the overall tone becomes more familiar and casual. Van Zandt thinks the writer may be suggesting a personal acquaintance with John Ramsey.

10—With its connotations of revolution, the closing 'Victory!'-harks back to the connection to foreign powers. 'S.B.T.C' may be another attempt to sound foreign, says Van Zandt.

In December of 2006, to mark a full decade since JonBenet had been killed, several forensic and behavioral experts were asked by the supermarket tabloid "Globe" to weigh in. One of them was Robert K. Ressler, founder of the FBI Behavioral Sciences Unit. He echoed many of DePue's sentiments, saying that "it's absolutely phony. Usually, a ransom note just gives the basics. But this one was full of colorful language and mixed messages. Then there's the matter of why any kidnapper would demand money when the victim's dead body was left behind. There's an almost maternal quality to comments like, 'the delivery will be exhausting so I advise you to be rested. A hardened criminal would never use those terms. He also noted that the acronym at the bottom of the note was done with periods between each letter, as was "FBI." Putting periods between letters in acronyms is a grammatical touch that has not been standard since the late 1960s. Patsy was born on December 29, 1956 and would have been a kid learning her English lessons in school before then. In those turbulent times, many organizations came along with "alphabet soup" names, and none of them used periods. There was SDS—Students for Democratic Society; PLO—Palestinian Liberation Organization; NOI—Nation of Islam; SLA—Symbionese Liberation Army (the people who kidnapped Patty Hearst and made the term "Stockholm Syndrome" famous); and the list goes on and on. Patsy was known to sign her letters to friends with acronyms with periods in them. One that stood out was "To B.V.F.M.F.A. from P.P.R.B.S.J." That meant "To Barbara V. Fernie, Master of Fine Arts from Patricia Paugh Ramsey, Bachelor of Science in Journalism." Patsy Ramsey had graduated college as a journalism major. She knew how to write a good story, and the note, as written, contained an opening that was properly set off from the body of the ransom letter, the way we were all taught to compose a letter. "Mr. Ramsey" is set off in a way that "Dear John" would be. Also, the closing line "Victory! S.B.T.C." was set off the way "Yours truly" would be rather than contained in the block of writing. Patsy Ramsey's writings from before and after the killing contain a large number of exclamation points, as does the ransom note. Not only that, but the reference to John Ramsey being a "fat cat," is also interesting. Not only was it a popular way for lefties to refer to rich people they see as evil or corrupt in the Sixties (some of them still do it), but from what I can gather, it was a nickname for John Ramsey, a rich corporate executive, that was used by Patsy's mother and father. Ressler also notes that the letter tells John to use his "good Southern common sense." John Ramsey is not from the American South. He originally comes from Michigan, near the Canadian border. Patsy Ramsey was born in West Virginia, right on the Mason-Dixon line, and lived for a long time in Atlanta, Georgia. Patsy's mother Nedra was often heard to say that John had "good Southern common sense" as a joke because he was a great businessman and for marrying her daughter, Patsy. Isn't that a coincidence?

Ressler also pointed out the use of the word "attaché." It's a word with French origins. It is usually spelled with the accent over the "e" to denote the sound of an "a." Patsy had studied French and lived in Atlanta, which has a strong undercurrent of French heritage. JonBenet's own name is a pseudo-French version of her father's first and middle names, John Bennett. It is always spelled with the accent over the second "e." Who else would bother with something like that? Lastly, concerning the ransom letter, DePue and Ressler and several others mentioned the $118,000 bonus that John Ramsey got at the end of the year. Who would know that except someone who was very familiar with John?

One of the questions that is often asked about this case is, "if they killed her and went to all the trouble to write a ransom letter, why didn't they get rid of the body?" That's simple: they couldn't. Even if you discount what the FBI said about parents having a harder time dumping a child's body out in the elements, they would have been spotted. Someone would have seen their car. They couldn't fly out to Florida because the pilot would have noticed JonBenet was dead. They couldn't have John fly (he has a pilot's license), because they had to meet the rest of the family in Michigan. Someone would have gotten hinky. But more than that, it goes back to what Kane said about Patsy soaking up the sympathy of being the grieving mother of a dead beauty queen combined with the ransom letter's emphasis on proper burial. The Ramseys went all out with JonBenet's funeral. It was a mega-event. All of their friends were there and so was the media. Patsy Ramsey made sure to dress in her finest, making sure she looked like Jacqueline Kennedy at President John Kennedy's funeral. In fact, that was how John Ramsey described her. As I said earlier, Patsy wanted to make JonBenet as spectacular in death as she was in life. It was JonBenet's greatest pageant, and Patsy's as well. To them, it wasn't a funeral. As an Internet sleuth with the screenname "voynich" put it, it was a wedding day with death, which is the best way I can think to put it.

How many coincidences are needed for one of those "hmmm!" moments, anyway? Quite a few, as I was to find out. Most of this was unknown to me from February 1997 to November 2001 and even beyond that time. In 1997, a picture of JonBenet in the now-legendary Showgirl outfit turned up and it showed JonBenet with a huge, angry-looking bruise on her arm. Her grandmother said that it was from an accident where a hamster cage fell on her. But at their presentation of evidence in June 1998, a photo of Patsy and JonBenet was shown where Patsy could be seen holding JonBenet's arm so hard that her fingernails were digging into the arm. Is that a coincidence?

John and Patsy Ramsey promised to find their daughter's killer. Apparently, they went to the OJ Simpson school of detective work: search all the right vacation spots, often leaving your remaining child unsupervised, where anybody and his cousin could get to him, all the while trying to shift blame onto the police. Hey, it worked for "the Juice," why not again? One of the more striking episodes in their never-ending quest involved Tony Frost, editor-in-chief of the "GLOBE" tabloid. A lot of people don't like Mr. Frost, including the Ramseys, I'm sure. But Patsy's approach (perhaps suggested by Susan Stine) was to find the man's home phone number and call his wife claiming to be his mistress in order to ruin his marriage, maybe even spark an incident like that between Carlo and Connie in *The Godfather.* This display of utter dedication to one's murdered child is touching, don't you think? And, of course, we have John Ramsey admitting in court that it was all lies.

There's one more thing I should probably mention. In her 1998 interview, Patsy Ramsey said if she had it all to do over again, she'd have turned the house into a fortress. Well, that's not what happened. In the early part of 2001, supposedly the Ramseys' house in Atlanta was broken in to. I say supposedly because there doesn't seem to be anything to the story. To hear him tell it, John Ramsey came home and caught the guy in the act, but got locked in the bathroom by this thief. There is good reason to believe that this break-in was as phony as the first. Number one, John Ramsey claims the thief was able to get in because when he (John) left the house, he left the door unlocked. WHAT?! These people have tried for years to convince us that someone broke into their house and killed their daughter. I'm lucky enough that my home has never been invaded, but I know some people who were not as lucky as me. They all say the same thing: you NEVER leave your home unlocked again! They sure don't act like someone whose daughter was murdered by someone unknown. Number two, the "thief" only took Patsy's jewelry, and not even the real jewelry, just the K-Mart stuff. Number three, John's description of the "thief" is so ridiculous as to not even be worth laughing at. The "thief" came right out of the Susan Smith play book: a well-dressed, soft-spoken, light-skinned black man. He was never found, either. I guess practice does make perfect. I'm just glad the Ramseys decided not to stage anymore crimes after that. Number four, John's story about being pinned in the bathroom by this phantom, who is said to have tied the door closed with John's own necktie, while screaming like a girl is beyond foolish. I guess he forgot that bathroom doors open inward.

Any questions? Probably. And the subsequent chapters should answer many of them.

CHAPTER FOUR

The Pain Behind The Painted Smile

Okay, so far, I've done my best to give you the who, the when, the what, the where, and the how. Now we come to the crucial juncture: the why.

I touched on it earlier, but now I'm going to give it to you both barrels.

Before JonBenet's death, I never knew there was such a thing as beauty pageants for little children. Since her death, many documentaries have been done on the subject. Apparently, over the last thirty years or so, child beauty pageants have gone from being an obscure part of Southern subculture to a billion-dollar a year industry. My personal feelings aside, Patsy grew up in a pageant family. Her mother Nedra was a very domineering woman, and pushed her daughters to be the best pageant queens they could be. Patsy and her sister Pam were highly successful, but never reached the Miss America finals. When JonBenet was born, Nedra asserted herself again. "JonBenet will do those pageants," she said. I don't blame Patsy for what happened to her. Sure, I think she was nuts, but her mother made her that way.

Despite Nedra's assertiveness (read: pushy), Patsy and JonBenet seemed to have a lot of fun together, with the possible exception of the one time when JonBenet, tired from a marathon day of photo shooting, got a little bratty and kicked her mother's wrist because the shoes Patsy wanted her to wear were hurting her little feet. But one incident does not necessarily lead to hatred, especially with such a loving, forgiving girl. Patsy seemed to let it slide as well.

What could make a loving mother with an extremely heavy investment in her daughter's future, turn into a killer? Indeed, Patsy's investment, both financially and emotionally, in transforming her little one into her "mini-me" would seem to challenge the idea that she could ever kill JonBenet. But dreams have a tendency of disintegrating like the proverbial snowball in hell, and when a dream of this size collapses, the dreamer will sometimes have an emotionally unhealthy response. In this instance, it would have to be something that nothing, in Patsy's mind, could ever fix, something that would make her daughter "broken" in her mind. Something so awful, so vile, so disgusting, that just hearing about it produces shudders and revulsion.

Someone, some monster, had ruined JonBenet. Someone had killed her inside. Someone had molested her.

This is one of the ugliest areas of the entire case, not to mention the most contentious, which is a big reason why very few people who are casual observers of the case know of it. As awful as it is to think of this beautiful little angel as a victim of such a horrific crime, I think it is necessary to illustrate this point to see how a loving mother could become a killer. Here's how I got there.

During JonBenet's autopsy, Dr. John Meyer examined her vagina. Here's what he found, from the actual report:

> *"A 1 cm red-purple area of abrasion is located on the right posterolateral area of the 1x1 cm hymeneal orifice. The*

hymen itself is represented by a rim of tissue extending clockwise from between the 2:00 and 10:00 positions. The area of abrasion is present at approximately the 7:00 position and appears to involve the hymen and the distal right vaginal wall."

Okay, for you regular people, that means that JonBenet's hymen was scratched. It has been established that her vagina was violated the night of her death. But the "1x1 cm hymeneal orifice" is the bell-ringer here. That means that the opening in JonBenet's six-year-old hymen was one centimeter by one centimeter. This is twice the size of a so-called normal hymeneal opening for a girl this age. In a September 1999 study for the Medical Journal *Family Medicine* titled "Genital Findings in Prepubertal Girls Evaluated for Sexual Abuse: A Different Perspective on Hymeneal Measurements," Dr. Perry Pugno said:

"Girls with no definitive signs of genital trauma exhibited a mean transhymenal diameter of 2.3 mm and in general showed an increase of approximately 1 mm per year of age. Girls with definitive signs of genital trauma exhibited a mean transhymenal diameter of 9.0 mm and no significant variance with age. Correcting for age differences, the transhymenal diameter was highly significant as a differentiating factor (F=1079, P<.001). When compared against the criterion standard, the transhymenal measurement is 99% specific and 79% sensitive as a screening tool."

These findings imply an "expected" hymeneal opening size of 6 mm for someone JonBenet's age; her actual opening size, 1 cm, placed her in the mid-range of sizes observed in this study among six-year olds known to have been abused. In fact, hymeneal sizes alone are not enough to say with any degree of certainty that JonBenet was the victim of long-term sexual abuse, but the autopsy report shows more than just hymeneal damage. Again, from the report:

> *"Vaginal Mucosa: All of the sections contain vascular congestion and focal interstitial chronic inflammation. The smallest piece of tissue, from the 7:00 position of the wall/hymen, contains epithelial erosion with underlying capillary congestion. A small number of red blood cells is present on the eroded surface. Acute inflammatory infiltrate is not seen."*

Go back and read that again. Let's take that one step at a time. "Chronic inflammation." That's a big one. Inflammation refers to an irritation that may involve pain, redness, heat (thus the term) and swelling. Here, take your fingernails and scratch your arm. Did you see how the skin became red? That's because the blood has come to the surface to heal the injury. This is known as acute inflammation. That means that JonBenet's vagina was injured or irritated and her body's systems went to work to try and heal her. It's the chronic part that seals the deal. The Bantam Medical Dictionary defines "chronic" as a disease or injury of long duration, and states that when healing does not occur, inflammation becomes chronic. In plain English, that means that JonBenet had old inflammation that had not been allowed to heal. This did not happen all at once. Even more damning is the term "erosion." No point in trying to obfuscate the issue: that means that layers of flesh in JonBenet's vagina had been worn away over time; stripped away by continuous invasion. Old and new vaginal injuries. It couldn't be any plainer than that.

But just in case it isn't plain yet, there are other findings that may prove equally interesting. One of the first professionals to state publicly that JonBenet was a victim of prolonged sexual (or at least vaginal) abuse was forensic pathologist Cyril Wecht. In his book, *Who Killed JonBenet,*" Wecht outlines his feelings. He was contacted by the supermarket tabloid magazine "The Globe" to review the case in early 1997. As he paid attention to the case and read the portion of the autopsy report that was released, he noted items that supported the likelihood of chronic sexual abuse—that is, her vaginal injury had not occurred at the time of the crime. It may have been done by a finger or some object, not via outright rape, but he believed it was clear that before the murder someone had behaved inappropriately with the child. "I have learned that the police called in three separate child sexual abuse experts," he reported. "They separately and independently came to the same conclusion that there was evidence of prior sexual abuse. But it's the most ridiculous thing in the world, a little girl with half of the hymen gone and she's dead, and you've got a tiny abrasion, a tiny contusion and a chronic inflammation of vaginal mucosa. That means it happened more than 72 hours earlier; we don't know how long, or how often it was repeated, but chronic means it wasn't from that night. This was a tragic, tragic accident."

It's easy enough to dismiss Wecht's analysis. After all, it was brought about by the interference of a tabloid, so that raises some interesting questions as to credibility. But he is not alone.

In his book, Det. Thomas states:

> *"In mid-September, a panel of pediatric experts from around the country reached one of the major conclusions of the investigation–that JonBenet had suffered vaginal trauma prior to the day she was killed. There were no dissenting opinions among them on the issue, and they firmly rejected any possibility that the trauma to the hymen and chronic vaginal inflammation were caused by urination issues or masturbation. We gathered affidavits stating in clear language that there were injuries 'consistent with prior trauma and sexual abuse' ' There was chronic abuse'. . . 'Past violation of the vagina'. . .'Evidence of both acute and injury and chronic sexual abuse.' In other words, the doctors were saying it had happened before."*

Thomas does not name these experts. But other sources, including Schiller's book, do name them. Their names read as follows:

- Dr. James Monteleone, Professor of Pediatrics at St. Louis University School of Medicine (and Director of Child Protection Cardinal Glennon Children's Hospital);
- Dr. David Jones, Professor of Preventative Medicine and Biometrics at University of Colorado Health Sciences Center;
- Dr. Ronald Wright, former Medical Examiner, Cook County Illinois;
- Dr. Virginia Rau of Dade County, Florida; and Dr. John McCann, Clinical Professor of Medicine, Department. of Pediatrics at University of California at Davis.

McCann is considered by many to be the world's leading authority on child sexual abuse. In fact, he was instrumental in establishing the proper methods and findings for determining child sexual abuse. His findings have been crucial in preventing misdiagnosis of child sexual abuse, such as happened in the McMartin trial. Since then, law enforcement officials have been anxious to avoid a repeat of that unfortunate incident.

McCann was contacted in mid-1997 to give a report for the police department. His findings were written down in the police reports and later transcribed by Bonita Sauer, a Denver legal secretary:

"According to McCann, examination findings that indicate chronic sexual abuse include the thickness of the rim of the hymen, irregularity of the edge of the hymen, the width or narrowness of the wall of the hymen, and exposure of structures of the vagina normally covered by the hymen. His report stated that there was evidence of prior hymeneal trauma as all of these criteria were seen in the post mortem examination of JonBenet.

"There was a three dimensional thickening from inside to outside on the inferior hymeneal rim with a bruise apparent on the external surface of the hymen and a narrowing of the hymeneal rim from the edge of the hymen to where it attaches to the muscular portion of the vaginal openings. At the narrowing area, there appeared to be very little if any hymen present. There was also exposure of the vaginal rugae, a structure of the vagina which is normally covered by an intact hymen. The hymeneal orifice measured one centimeter which is abnormal or unusual for this particular age group and is further evidence of prior sexual abuse with a more recent injury as shown by the bruised area on the inferior hymeneal rim. A generalized increase in redness of the tissues of the vestibule was apparent, and small red flecks of blood were visible around the perineum and the external surface of the genitalia." He also talked about the injury from that night, saying, "the injury appeared to have been caused by a relatively small, very firm object which, due to the area of bruising, had made very forceful contact not only with the hymen, but also with the tissues surrounding the hymen. McCann believed that the object was forcefully jabbed in – not just shoved in. Although the bruised area would indicate something about the size of a finger nail, he did not believe it was a finger, because of the well demarcated edges of the bruise indicating an object much firmer than a finger. McCann also noted that in children of this age group the labia, or vaginal lips, remain closed until literally manually separated. In order for there to be an injury to the hymen without injuring the labia, the labia would have to be manually separated before the object was inserted. The examination also indicated that the assault was done while the child was still alive because of the redness in the surrounding tissue and blood in the area. McCann stated that this injury would have been very painful because the area of the injury as indicated by the bruise was at the base of the hymen were most of the nerve endings are located. Such an injury would have caused a six year old child to scream or yell. The doctor also stated that he assumed the object did not have jagged edges because there were no evidence of tears in the bruised area." To qualify his report, Dr. McCann explained "the term 'chronic abuse' meant only that it was 'repeated', but that the number of incidents could not be determined. In the case of JonBenet, the doctor could only say that there was evidence of 'prior abuse'. The examination results were evidence that there was at least one prior penetration of the vagina through the hymeneal membrane. The change in the hymeneal structure is due to healing from a prior penetration. However, it was not possible to determine neither the number of incidents nor over what period of time. Because the prior injury had healed, any other incidents of abuse probably were more than 10 days prior." He explained that the most common perpetrators of sexual abuse are those with whom the child has close contact with, usually a family member. Increased bedwetting is also a possible sign, he said.

Dr. Richard Krugman, Dean of the University of Colorado Medical School and Dr. Andrew Sirotnak of the Denver Children's Hospital weighed in. Krugman had been brought in by the DA's office. Sirotnak had attended the autopsy itself. In 2001, they co-authored a medical treatise on child abuse using JonBenet as a kickoff point. That pretty much tells you where they came down on it.

Dr. Robert Kirschner, from the University of Chicago, Department of Pathology, weighed in as well. In a 1997 article for *Vanity Fair* magazine written by Ann Bardach, he stated:

> "The vaginal opening, according to Dr. Robert Kirschner of the University of Chicago's pathology department, was twice the normal size for six-year-olds. The genital injuries indicate penetration," he says, "but probably not by a penis, and are evidence of molestation that night as well as previous molestation." "If she had been taken to a hospital emergency room, and doctors had seen the genital evidence, her father would have been arrested"

Lastly, Thomas writes in his book that, during an evidence presentation in June 1998, Det. Jane Harmer gave the gathered group an anatomy lesson. She showed side-by-side photographs of JonBenet's vagina and that of a normal six-year-old girl. "Even to the uninitiated, the visual difference was apparent."

Well, there it is in black and white. McCann, Jones, Monteleone, Wright, Krugman, and a pathologist named Werner Spitz did not just examine the report and autopsy photographs of JonBenet's vagina. The most important evidence came from tissue slides. These professionals examined samples of tissue cut from JonBenet's vagina under a microscope, to be extra sure. As Det. Thomas states, "there were no dissenting opinions." Some years later in 2001, several other physicians came forward with opinions. One was forensic pathologist Dr. Robert Goldberg. After Goldberg reviewed JonBenet's autopsy report, he told GLOBE: "There were new vaginal injuries over old ones. The tissue was stretched and eroded, not just torn. This happens over time. JonBenet's hymenal opening was roughly twice that of an unmolested child."

I should mention that the physical findings alone are not the only red-flags that are thrown up by JonBenet. It is well-known that she had regressed in her toilet training. About the time Patsy got sick, little JonBenet became terrified that her mommy might die. Her toilet training regressed to that of an infant. She was a frequent bed wetter, and would even wet herself during the day, requiring a change of panties. She would often ask any nearby adult to change and wipe her. But even after Patsy recovered, it didn't get much better. JonBenet was reduced to wearing training pants like a toddler. By the time of her death, the regression had taken on a new dimension: soiling. Linda Hoffmann-Pugh stated that she once found JonBenet laying in her own filth. In 2006, FOX

News did an interview with Holly Smith. At the time of JonBenet's murder, she was the head of the Boulder County Sex Abuse team. In the interview, she talked about what she found. "There is this dynamic of children that have been sexually abused sometimes soiling themselves or urinating in their beds to keep someone who is hurting them at bay," explains Smith....While Smith points out there could be innocent explanations, this was the kind of information that raised questions. Hoping to zero in on a possibility, Smith said that by the third day of the investigation, she'd found fecal staining on every pair of JonBenet's panties. I'm not talking simple "skid marks." These clothing items had been laundered beforehand.

When I first caught wind of this case, I was puzzled by the pageant videos of JonBenet done up like a Vegas showgirl and parading around like one. I'd often heard that children who were being sexually abused would act out in a sexual manner. I wondered, but I later found out that it was and is standard for child beauty pageant participants to do that. As it turned out, Patsy's friend Pam Griffin had a teenage daughter who had been in pageants herself and had taught JonBenet those moves. It would be several years before I learned the awful truth. And it is awful.

When something like this happens, people tend to go crazy. We all have our mental image of pedophiles: the dirty old man down the street, the guy in dark glasses offering candy, and all of those other stereotypes. We're always shocked when it turns out to be a relative, a trusted friend, a known baby-sitter, or a friendly teacher. It's even more sickening to realize that when a child is molested, a family member is often the culprit. What's most shocking of all is that it often goes undetected. It's difficult enough for adult women to admit that they were raped. One estimate is that as much as sixty percent of all rapes go unreported. Rape is known in some circles as the only crime where the victim can be victimized twice: first during the actual act and then having to relive it by testifying in court and being raked over the coals by defense attorneys. It's just too traumatic to relive, and a lot of women just do not wish to subject themselves to it. Well, now imagine what it must be like for a little child. They don't always know it's wrong, especially if their victimizer is a trusted adult. They are exceptionally easy to manipulate and control through fear or bribery. And most of them want only to please adults, which plays into factors one and two. JonBenet would have been an ideal victim for a molester: beautiful, charming, and trained to obey adults. Patsy and her mother Nedra had very little tolerance for disobedience.

Now, just imagine that JonBenet had blurted all of this out to Patsy, as she is supposed to have done in my theory of the crime. Patsy's worn out, tired, irritated and definitely not in the mood to hear something like that, but it doesn't matter, because that is the kind of thing that nobody wants to hear under any circumstances, especially since she had so much invested in JonBenet.

Patsy may have had a low set point to begin with. Bear in mind that my feelings are based only on distant observation, but some of her mannerisms suggest a woman hiding a serious trauma. In 1998, she was interviewed by retired Denver homicide detective Tom Haney. When he brought up the medical findings, things became very interesting:

TOM HANEY: Okay. Ms. Ramsey, are you aware that there had been prior vaginal intrusion on JonBenet?

PATSY RAMSEY: No, I am not. Prior to the night she was killed?

TOM HANEY: Correct.

PATSY RAMSEY: No, I am not.

TOM HANEY: Didn't know that?

1PATSY RAMSEY: No, I didn't.

TOM HANEY: Does that surprise you?

PATSY RAMSEY: Extremely.

TOM HANEY: Does that shock you?

PATSY RAMSEY: It shocks me.

TOM HANEY: Does it bother you?

PATSY RAMSEY: Yes, it does.

TOM HANEY: Who, how could she have been violated like that?

PATSY RAMSEY: I don't know. This is the absolute first time I ever heard that.

TOM HANEY: Take a minute, if you would, I mean this seems —you know, you didn't know that before right now, the 25th, at 2:32?

PATSY RAMSEY: No, I absolutely did not.

TOM HANEY: Okay. Does–

PATSY RAMSEY: And I would like to see where it says that and who reported that.

TOM HANEY: Okay.

PATSY RAMSEY: Well, can you find that?

TOM HANEY: Yeah. Because I think it's pretty significant?

PATSY RAMSEY: I think it's damn significant. You know, I am shocked.

TOM HANEY: And based on the reliable medical information that we have at this point, that is a fact.

PATSY RAMSEY: Now when you say violated, what are you —what are you telling me here?

TOM HANEY: That there was some prior vaginal intrusion that something —something was inserted

PATSY RAMSEY: Prior to this night that she was assaulted?

TOM HANEY: That's the–

PATSY RAMSEY: What report as —I want to see, I want to see what you're talking about here. I am —I am —I don't —I am shocked.

TOM HANEY: Well, that's one of the things that's been bothering us about the case.

PATSY RAMSEY: No damn kidding.

TOM HANEY: What does that tell you?

PATSY RAMSEY: It doesn't tell me anything!

It doesn't tell her anything. If any of you reading this are mothers, I'm sure it would mean a lot to you. This transcript really does not do justice to what really happened. If you've never seen the videotape of this segment, you are really missing out: Patsy, for all of her proclaiming to be shocked, is as cold as a rattlesnake in the middle of winter; a real popsicle. But then it takes a turn for the worse:

TOM HANEY: And prior to today, had you heard or read or seen anything about–

PATSY RAMSEY: I had heard that the night she was killed that she may have had —have been sexually assaulted. But not prior to that. Absolutely.

TOM HANEY: Have you ever suffered any physical abuse?

PATSY RAMSEY: Absolutely not.

TOM HANEY: In childhood, you know, dating, your adult life?

PATSY RAMSEY: (NO AUDIBLE RESPONSE).

TOM HANEY: How about sexual abuse?

PATSY RAMSEY: (NO AUDIBLE RESPONSE).

And at that point, he asks her if anyone in her family ever told her they had been abused. But look again: she answers him so low no one could hear what she said. Her whole demeanor changed. Up to the point where he asked her if she'd ever been abused, she was in kind of a "can-we-move-this-along" mood. But upon being asked if she was ever abused as a child, she becomes a frightened little girl. I thought she'd cry when I saw the video. Maybe she would have, but didn't want to give them the satisfaction. Det. Thomas says in his book that Haney told him, "she's not a very good actress." I don't know. He may have nailed her on something. If she was abused in her past, she would definitely have a pronounced reaction to JonBenet telling her.

That's the kind of thing you try to forget and pretend never happened. JonBenet's off-the-cuff remark, while perhaps meaning little to a child, would mean a great deal to Patsy, a virtual hammer crushing her to powder inside. Her first instinct would be to deny it. The idea that it could happen to JonBenet would be shattering. In the scenario I outlined, Patsy reacted with extreme rage. She took refuge in the idea that JonBenet was lying. Maybe she had picked up something from one of her friends or an older kid, like one of Burke's friends. Anything to keep from facing the awful truth: that as a victim of abuse who was suppressing the memory, she was more likely to marry someone who was also an abuser and she subconsciously blamed herself for not protecting her daughter. At that point, Patsy would have sought to shut JonBenet's lying mouth. And when it became clear that she had done the unthinkable, she turned her fury on the cause of the problem. And perhaps later she convinced herself that JonBenet had been wrong. Maybe she was lying, or just mistaken, or had ideas put in her head by someone else. It would just be too painful to both lose your daughter AND find out that you killed the wrong person. Patsy claimed in an interview with Barbara Walters in 2000 that if she had any inkling that John was abusing JonBenet, she'd have, quote, "knocked his block off." That's certainly a mature, credible way of phrasing it. Come ON, Patsy! "Knocked his block off?" Who are you, Jiminy Cricket? That's something you say when your husband burns the toast. You could have at least said, "I'd have killed the bastard." Well, regardless, perhaps she tried. In my scenario, she did attack him. Also, in an interview for the "National Enquirer" tabloid in 2000, Patsy confessed that she had considered the possibility of John molesting JonBenet during her cancer treatments, but wrote it off. Her reasoning for doing so was very odd. She didn't consider it, then dismiss it because "oh, he'd never do something like that." She dismissed it because her mother was sleeping inside the room like a guard dog. Why did Nedra have to keep watch in the first place, is my question..

What kind of person did Patsy get involved with, anyway?

In the 1800s, an Austrian psychologist named Richard von Krafft-Ebing determined that there were three kinds of people who victimized children sexually. The first kind are pedophiles. In the true sense, this applies to people who have recurring sexual attractions and urges toward children; no one really knows why they do this. I think it's just cross-wiring of the brain. The second kind are situational or surrogate molesters. These are people who are not sexually attracted to children as such, but see a child as a substitute for an adult object of attraction, for example, a woman who molests her son because her husband walked out on her. The third kind are sadistic molesters. These ungodly specimens get a sexual thrill from inflicting pain on their victims, physical and emotional. A sadistic child molester, like a situational molester, does not have any specific attraction to children, but selects them for victimization only because children are easier to terrify and control. The thrill is intensified through this factor.

Now, as you saw in Chapter Three, I believe that John, if not JonBenet's actual molester, was blamed for it by Patsy, at least at first. Let me be very clear on something: I cannot say with 100% certainty that he was the doer. Just because JonBenet was molested doesn't necessarily mean he did it, or even knew about it. Any evidence I present to that effect is purely circumstantial. However, when I take everything together, I have good reason to believe he was the one responsible. In the interviews in 2000, the DA's representatives dropped a real bombshell on John. They told him that fibers from the Israeli-made black shirt he was wearing at Fleet White's party were found in JonBenet's underwear. Since the shirt was a dry-clean-only item, and since the underwear JonBenet had on were fresh from the package, per Patsy's statements, that pretty much killed any possibility of an innocent transfer to the panties in the laundry. The bell was tolling, and John did not need to ask for whom. So he said the only thing that came into his mind:

"BULLSHIT!" And then he began to hem and haw, getting progressively more flustered. It's one of those moments that Kodak was meant for. As the credit card commercials say, "priceless." He nearly shit his pants! Luckily for him, Lin Wood stepped in. More about him later on.

Wood later tried to claim that this was a lie and he knew it was a lie. He didn't say this to the prosecutors, but on *Larry King Live* with no one to challenge him. His implication was clear: he was trying to cloud the issue by reminding people that police officers can indeed lie to suspects during an interrogation to induce confessions. True, police officers can do that. But this was not a police station and these were lawyers, not cops. Perhaps Mr. Wood is not familiar with Colorado law, since he is based from Atlanta, so I'll give him and all of you reading this a little civics lesson:

> *Colorado Rules of Professional Conduct : Rule 4.1 Truthfulness in Statements to Others "In the course of representing a client a lawyer shall not knowingly: a) make a false or misleading statement of fact or law to a third person; or (b) fail to disclose a material fact to a third person when disclosure is necessary to avoid assisting a*

> *criminal or fraudulent act by a client, unless disclosure is prohibited by Rule 1.6. COMMENT Misrepresentation A lawyer is required to be truthful when dealing with others on a client's behalf, but generally has no affirmative duty to inform an opposing party of relevant facts. A misrepresentation can occur if the lawyer incorporates or affirms a statement of another person that the lawyer knows is false. Misrepresentations can also occur by failure to act."*

For those of you who do not understand legalese, this means that if Kane, Levin and Morrissey were stupid enough to do what Wood suggests, they might face any number of reprimands up to an including having their law licenses revoked. That's just something to keep in mind.

Sort of got caught with your hands in the cookie jar, John?

But it didn't end there. 2000 was a hit and a half for John. That year, former Boulder Police Detective Linda Arndt, the one who let John and Fleet root around in the basement, was deposed in a civil suit she'd brought against the city. Here's what she had to say:

Q: *Which opinions were these?*

A: *Incest, naming the Ramseys as suspects.*

Q: *This is incest between John Ramsey and JonBenet?*

A: *Yes, to the whole incest dynamic in the family.*

Q: *But involving John Ramsey and JonBenet, any other members?*

A: *Well, specifically because she's the one who's dead.*

Q: *But when you refer again to incest, it could involve any number of family members. I'm just trying to identify the family members when you use that term.*

A: *Well, there's a whole dynamic, because everybody's got a role in the family.*

Q: *The incest has an effect on family members, does it not?*

A: *Well, in general terms that covers it when you talk about an act, but I'm talking about the dynamic.*

Q: *I understand about the dynamic, but I want to get the predicate first. The participants in the incest, when you refer to incest, you're referring to John Ramsey and JonBenet and no other family members?*

A: *I refer to every member of the family. Every member has a role.*

Q: *But in terms of the sexual act that's implicit in the term of "incest," you're referring to John Ramsey and JonBenet?*

A: *Yes*

In an interview for "Good Morning America" on the ABC network in 1999, Arndt, who had been present at JonBenet's autopsy, said that the coroner told her that JonBenet was the victim of sexual molestation, but he wouldn't go on record unless called into court.

Lastly, John's attitude toward the issue of molestation is troubling, to say the least. When Det. Thomas mentioned the expert panel on Larry King Live, I thought John was going to reach across the table and belt him, walk off the set, or both. And why does Patsy always smile when the question is broached? Did she think this was some kind of game?

You have to wonder why someone would stick by their man when it turns out he's the worst kind of victimizer. Well, perhaps she blamed herself, as I mentioned. I don't think John falls into Dr. von Krafft-Ebing's first category, if for no other reason than he raised two daughters who never had anything bad to say about him. Besides, the cookie jar John's first wife caught him with his hand in had all of her wisdom teeth. Most people who aren't familiar with the case don't know that John had a first wife, Lucinda. She's still around. He cheated on her, he got caught, she got a lawyer. We men always get caught, because we think we won't. Make no mistake: Patsy was not the other woman. He didn't marry his mistress. According to television guru Dr. Phil McGraw, most marriages that start out as affairs don't last long.. John had been divorced for several years before he met Patsy. From what I hear it was love at first sight. He always called her his "trophy wife," a reference to her beauty pageant days. Still, I believe Beth's death changed him, and for the worse. To this day, he maintains that the death of Elizabeth, which was a car accident in 1992, was and is more painful to him than the active killing of JonBenet. He even keeps a picture of Beth in his bathroom. And even though he seems to get the warm fuzzies (and a look on his face like a cat toying with a mouse) when he talks about suing Det. Thomas on the aforementioned Larry King episode, I seriously doubt he falls into number three, either. So that leaves number two. One has to remember that Patsy's temporary victory over ovarian cancer came with a price tag: operations that rendered sexual activity difficult. Enter JonBenet, prancing around in those showgirl outfits, expertly put together by her mother. In his starved brain, he may have thought, "Patsy is saying 'here she is. She's all yours. I've prepared her for you.'" JonBenet was "safe." She wasn't old enough to get life-destroying cancer, and she wasn't old enough to get herself killed driving a car. She was easy to manipulate and control, a perfect "playmate." When she wound up dead, he knew the implications. People who abuse kids don't fare too well in prison. So they had to hide it. Jamming a paintbrush into your daughter's vagina, family of the year material right there.

I should talk about that. Aside from her previous injuries, JonBenet had vaginal injuries from the night she was killed as well. Her injuries have been described as "consistent with digital penetration." That means it's possible that someone stuck their finger(s) in JonBenet's vagina. But remember what John McCann said. He said that it was more likely that something harder was used. Since a shard of wood from the paintbrush that was used as the handle of the garrote was found inside her, it's likely that it was used as the instrument to penetrate her. The end of the brush was never found. Since the brush was broken off, as evidenced by the sharp, rough ends, it's most probable that it was jabbed into her with the handle end still intact and smooth, then broken off. The brush as seen would have caused far more damage to JonBenet's insides. Only a few drops of blood were found in JonBenet's underwear. This is significant for two reasons: one, it says that the penetration was only half-hearted. Two, because there wasn't more blood, it shows that JonBenet's insides had toughened up due to past violations, according to the late Dr. Judianne Densen-Gerber, a forensic psychologist. In Schiller's book, the CASKU agents weighed in on the injuries from that night, saying:

> "The sexual violation of JonBenet, whether pre or postmortem did not appear to have been committed for the perpetrators gratification. The penetration, which caused minor genital trauma, was more likely part of a staged crime scene intended to mislead the police."

Whether the brush was used for this purpose or not is debated. I believe it was.

In 2000, Dr. Werner Spitz was asked his opinion by a Michigan newspaper. He said, quote: "Someone took a lot of time to stage strangulation and sexual assault."

There was something else, too: JonBenet's clothes. She had been redressed. Her pants had been pulled back up. What sadistic-control pedophile killer would do that?

On any number of Web sites, you can encounter sick humor related to this case similar to the television program "Family Guy." One is pictures of JonBenet arranged like a comic book, complete with word balloons. She says, "at least I didn't die a virgin. Thanks, Daddy!" Ugh. Draw your own conclusions.

In all of this mess, there's only one person who challenges the notion that JonBenet was being sexually abused: her pediatrician, Dr. Francesco Beuf. But he's hardly a credible source, since he admits he never conducted an internal exam, which is absolutely necessary to determine these things. Also, his records of JonBenet's medical history seem to have vanished into thin air. Beuf was, and to my knowledge still is, friends with the Ramsey family. This may have clouded his judgment, as would the possibility of him losing his license to practice medicine if he DID suspect something and didn't follow up on it. So that pretty much lets him out as any kind of authority.

Right now, you're probably asking yourself, "how could this woman stay with a husband who was doing these things? No choice. She had to save her son and there was too much evidence against her. The best insurance in the world is another suspect. You can't charge one because they will try to stick the blame on the other. Like it or not, you're stuck with them for the rest of your life. With Patsy dead, the only person who could have done John in is gone. That's the trouble with trying to get into people's heads. Sometimes you come out feeling like no amount of showering in the world will get you clean again.

CHAPTER FIVE

A Little Bowl of Pineapple and a Table Full of Lies

Now, we are going to examine three key points that should have sealed the Ramseys' fate. We'll start with a basic food item.

In the autopsy report, JonBenet's intestine was explored. Inside was a greenish substance that could have been digested plant material such as fruit or vegetables. As Det. Thomas and Det. Smit later confirmed, it was, in fact, pineapple, the same kind that was found in the bowl on the counter of the Ramsey home kitchen. In *Perfect Murder, Perfect Town*, the coroner's report said that the pineapple was in "near-perfect condition" with "sharp edges" and appeared to have been "poorly chewed." The pineapple in the bowl was fresh, not canned. Smit told John Ramsey in 1998 that it was a "big bugaboo."

The average rate of digestion for pineapple is two hours. It can take as little as one-and-one-half hours, or as long as three hours. This can be affected by the person's metabolism or any illnesses they might have. To narrow it down, the police investigated what JonBenet might have eaten that day. According to Fleet and Priscilla White, they did not serve pineapple at their party on Christmas night. They did serve cracked crab, and apparently, JonBenet liked it enough to ask to take some home. Fleet White obliged. Now, by most accounts, JonBenet didn't eat very much at the party. So it's likely that whatever she had eaten was already processed by the time of her death, since no cracked crab was found.

Now, the Ramseys have always said that JonBenet fell asleep in the car on the way home and remained asleep until she was killed. Oddly, in an early interview, Burke Ramsey told the authorities that JonBenet was awake and walked up the stairs ahead of him. He later recanted. I wonder why. But the pineapple is important because it puts the lie to the idea that JonBenet was asleep. The Ramseys arrived home at 10:00 PM. Dr. Werner Spitz estimated the time of death as around 1:00 AM. That means that JonBenet had to have eaten the pineapple after she got home. Since the only fingerprints found on the bowl and spoon belonged to Patsy and Burke, JonBenet didn't get to it herself. She couldn't reach the top of the counter, so she'd need to climb on something to reach it, but nothing was out of place. None of the kitchen chairs were moved. So, someone had to get it for her. This is the big lie the Ramseys were caught in. To this day, they contend that no one in the house fed it to her, and even they can't swallow the idea that an intruder gave it to her, then waited the two hours for it to digest before he killed her. If they had just said, "yes, we gave her some as a bedtime snack," that would have been the end of it. Only one parent would have to know. When I was a kid, my dad would give his two boys a piece of candy every now and then, saying, "here, fellas. Don't tell your mother." And we never did! But, since they had already told the cops that JonBenet was asleep and never woke up, thus they couldn't have fed her anything, their rice was already fried. During the 1998 interviews, the first day John Ramsey was interviewed, he said that no one fed JonBenet pineapple under any circumstances, since she wouldn't have eaten it from an intruder anyway. Det. Thomas writes in his book, quote:

> "The very next day he retracted that firm statement, saying his lawyer chastised him for making it. Neither he nor Patsy fed her pineapple, he said, but then he asked, 'What if she knew the intruder?' After thinking about it, he said, 'It hit me like a ton of bricks.' JonBenet 'adored' Santa Bill McReynolds, and if he had come into her room, she would have gotten out of bed and gone downstairs with him without a problem. 'She may have had a secretly prearranged meeting.' he said. 'Maybe he fed her pineapple.' The detectives stopped the tape and watched that section repeatedly. Only the day before, Ramsey had said such a thing was impossible. Now he laid it on Santa Bill."

Does anyone else smell burning pants?

Another wrinkle is in JonBenet's hands, literally. On the palm of one hand was drawn a heart in red ink. In 1998, "Trip" DeMuth asked Patsy about it. She said that it was very well-drawn. He asked where it might have come from. Patsy said that JonBenet had a habit of drawing on herself, and that Patsy tried to discourage her from doing that because of pageants. She claimed that drawing hearts on hands was something JonBenet and Daphne White liked to do with each other.

The next day, Patsy was asked about it again. This time, she gave a much different answer, saying that she hadn't actually seen the heart, and couldn't say for sure whether or not she'd just read about it or heard about it, didn't prevent her going into detail the first time. One book posits this claim: "*One of Patsy's friends recently revealed that Patsy often drew a heart in JonBenet's palm and told her, "While you are asleep you have my heart in your hand and you don't have to be scared." Someone who knows the Ramseys well said that "JonBenet herself never made such drawings on her palm-only Patsy did.*" A Mother Gone Bad: The Hidden Confession of JonBenet's Killer, by Dr. Andrew Hodges, 1998

They say the third time's a charm. Boy, the Boulder police department found that out the hard way. Patsy Ramsey's 911 call was recorded, as per operating procedure, but when the police listened to it, they thought they could hear something right before the hang-up. They couldn't tell what it was, but it was worth checking out. They sent the tape to the FBI lab for enhancement, but the Feds didn't have equipment that was advanced enough to lift anything. The police tried the United States Secret Service, but they had the same problem. Finally, they got wind of a technology firm in El Segundo, California called the Aerospace Corporation. Supposedly, they were on the cutting edge of modern technology, so the police gave them a go. What came back was extremely interesting. Just before the hang-up, a voice that turned out to be Burke Ramsey could be heard asking, "what is it? What did you find?" Detective Melissa Hickman brought the tape back and they all had a listen. A full transcript is available in Schiller's *Perfect Murder, Perfect Town* and Steve Thomas's *JonBenet: Inside The Ramsey Murder Investigation*, so here it is again:

Patsy: "Police."

911: "What's going on ma'am?"

Patsy: "755 15th street."

911: "What's going on there ma'am"

Patsy: "We have a kidnapping. Hurry, please!"

911: "Explain to me what's going on. OK?"

Patsy: "There. We have a, there's a note left and our daughter's gone."

911: "A note was left and your daughter's gone?"

Patsy: "Yes!"

911: "How old is your daughter?"

Patsy: "She's 6 years old. She's blonde, 6 years old."

911: "How long ago was this?"

Patsy: "I don't know I just got the note, and my daughter's gone."

911: "Does it say who took her?"

Patsy: "What?"

911: "Does it say who took her?"

Patsy: "No! I don't know. There's a, there's a ransom note here."

911: "It's a ransom note?"

Patsy: "It says SBTC. Victory! Please!"

911: "Okay, what's your name? Are you Kath...?"

Patsy: "Patsy Ramsey, I'm the mother. Oh my God! Please!"

911: "Okay, I'm sending an officer over OK?

Patsy: "Please!"

911: "Do you know how long she's been gone?"

Patsy: "No I don't! Please we just got up and she's not here. Oh my god! Please!"

911: "Okay, Cal...."

Patsy: "Please send somebody."

911: "I am honey."

Patsy: "Please."

911: "Take a deep breath and..."

Patsy: "Hurry, hurry, hurry!"

911: "Patsy? Patsy? Patsy? Patsy?"

At this point, Burke is heard asking, "Please, what do I do?"

John Ramsey responds in anger, saying, "we're not speaking to you!"

Patsy gasps out, "Help me, Jesus, help me, Jesus."

Finally, Burke says, What did you find?"

This is important because, just as they claimed that JonBenet was asleep when they got home, the Ramseys first stated that Burke was asleep during the 911 call and remained so until he was awakened and sent to the Whites' house. His voice on the tape suggests two things: it suggests that they were lying when they said he was asleep, and that since he was awake, Patsy's screaming woke him up and their story about not being able to hear screaming is also a lie.

Over time, the story about Burke being asleep has changed in fits and starts. In the interviews of June 1998, John Ramsey said he checked on Burke and found him asleep. Later, he said Burke was pretending to be asleep because he was scared. The changing story culminated in an interview between the Ramseys and the "National Enquirer" tabloid where John described Burke as awake, asking questions and so frightened he was crying. Sounds like they tried to cover all of their bases.

Lastly, the Ramseys and their supporters claim that JonBenet was taken from her room down the same spiral staircase Patsy descended in the morning. During a television broadcast on "A&E" host Bill Kurtis was led through the house, including down the spiral staircase. The thing was irritatingly noisy, creaking loudly with every step. You'd have to be in a coma not to hear it. If Bonita Sauer's transcriptions are to be believed, Burke Ramsey said he could hear someone opening the refrigerator door from his bedroom. The Ramseys have always maintained that they would not have been able to hear anything in their third floor bedroom, but since someone would have heard something in the dead of the night, and compared to their record of truth-telling, you've really got to wonder why we should believe them.

Okay, now take the pineapple, 911 tape, noisy house, the heart and the changing stories surrounding them. Then balance them against the Ramseys. They don't quite hold up, do they? These inconsistent stories have given rise to a term in the Internet subculture surrounding this case: "Ramnesia."

Lastly, JonBenet's grave marker says she died on December 25, 1996. Since the time of death was never nailed down 100%, you have to wonder why the Ramseys would put that date on there. Guilty conscience, perhaps?

That burning pants smell is starting to fill the room.

CHAPTER SIX

From Intruder to Mom & Dad; Why I Changed My Opinion on Who Killed JonBenet

To understand why I decided to write this book, you have to understand how I went from believing in Ramsey innocence to the horrible realization that they most likely killed their beautiful daughter. I've just outlined my personal theory and the evidence that leads me to develop it over time. Now, I'm going to give you the chronology of events as they happened to change my mind. A lot of people claim, in some cases sarcastically, that I "saw the light," a la Saint Paul on the Road to Damascus. But it didn't happen that way. It didn't happen all at once. It was slow and painful.

Think of a suit of armor like the knights wore in the late Middle Ages. It gives great protection, but over time it becomes rusted and dented the more it gets hammered on. That's how it happened with me. The first chink in the armor appeared when both Ramseys confronted Detective Steve Thomas on an episode of Larry King's talk show on May 31, 2000. The Ramseys, Thomas, and other players in the case had appeared on his program up to that point, but nothing could have prepared anyone for what would come. I hadn't paid much attention to the case for a while, but I had a fair idea of who Thomas was. To hear Team Ramsey (as he called them) put it, he was to the Ramsey case what Mark Fuhrman was to the OJ Simpson case. But it was the first time I saw the Ramseys for what they really were: manipulative narcissists who throw a hissy fit whenever anyone stands up to them. They refused to let Thomas make his points, and their behavior was troubling. Patsy had clearly been "preparing" for the confrontation, because she was clearly impaired through the use of some kind of drug. She was swaying, slurring her words, and could barely sit up straight. "Stoned off her ass" is the popular term for it. Not until Anna Nicole Smith's TV show would I ever again be treated to the sight of someone on TV being that medicated. The only real emotion that Patsy seemed capable of was bitchiness. I really don't mean to be so hard on her, but why she agreed to it in the first place is beyond me. The most precious moment came when Patsy touched Thomas's arm, saying what a good guy he could be and telling him they needed to work together to find the "real killer," as she pushed her breasts in his face, trying to seduce him, I guess. Meanwhile, John was sitting there the whole time smiling, which I later likened to the Emperor in *Star Wars*. He laughed at the most inappropriate things, compared JonBenet's death to killing a dog, and threatened to walk off the set when Thomas mentioned the findings of the sexual abuse experts. Clearly, Thomas got to him. Two days later, H. Ellis Armistead, the head private investigator working for the Ramseys quit. He cited "events taking place in the media," and implied that they were getting bad advice from their new lawyers, whom he did not get along with.

The second chink came almost exactly a year later, in May 2001. Lou Smit, who I will talk more about later, was doing what can only be likened to a traveling medicine show trying to prove his theory of an intruder. One of his points involved a demonstration of how he thought the intruder entered the house through a broken window that John Ramsey and Fleet White saw that morning. The photograph shows the window well that morning. The dirt and debris are completely undisturbed. In Smit's scenario, the intruder had to lift up the grate, step in, and slide through. Now, there are a few things wrong with this. First, no footprints were found in the dirt at all. Second, to avoid wiping the dirt off with his butt, the intruder would have to go in all at once, like a gymnast on the uneven parallel bars. That could not have happened.

Also, the window doesn't open all the way. It can only open part way out because of a pipe. Smit, a skinny man, was wearing no winter clothing when he demonstrated his scenario. Yet, he could only do it by dropping into the well, squatting, sticking his legs in, sliding around on his butt, and slipping in, during which he completely obliterated the dirt and leaves in the well. It just doesn't work. Steve Thomas said that he and several other detectives did this and they couldn't do it either. Worse than that, he claimed the intruder left the same way, climbing up onto a suitcase under the window and climbing out. His way out was even worse. To start with, the suitcase was not under the window when Fleet White found it. It was moved there later. No hand prints were found in the well, and no fibers were snagged on the frame. And he was supposed to have done this in the dark. This man had just shown me that the theory I subscribed to could not have happened. I respected this man. That would change, as well. I'm a regular guy. I believe my own eyes, and I can't not see what my eyes see. I don't have a "stupid" button that I can push to get stupid. It was a shaking experience to say the very least.

That November, John and Patsy Ramsey were deposed in a civil lawsuit. Two things came out of their sworn testimony that turned the chinks into huge dents. First, a chart was produced containing side-by-side comparisons of Patsy's handwriting to the handwriting on the ransom letter. It was shocking, to put it mildly. The second thing came during John's deposition, where he finally confessed that he had been lying for some time. He had always claimed that he had hired private investigators to follow up on leads the police wouldn't because, supposedly, they were too caught up trying to pin it on the Ramseys. In his deposition, he stated that the private eyes were only to help build a defense against any future prosecution against them. "To keep us out of jail," he said. John seemed as committed to finding the real killer as OJ Simpson. And on that note, it didn't help that those same private eyes were caught with their hands in the cookie jar earlier in the year. Tom Miller, a lawyer and court-approved handwriting expert, had gone to trial in July for allegedly trying to buy a copy of the ransom letter illegally. He had been tricked into a setup by a tabloid reporter. He was arrested and approached with a deal: the charges would be dropped if he were to surrender his law license and repudiate his own handwriting credentials. No self-respecting man in his position would take that deal. So, he went to trial in July 2001. At his trial, it came out that David L. Williams, a private investigator working for the Ramseys, had been working behind the scenes to dig up dirt on Tom Miller to use against him if he were ever called to testify against Patsy at trial. David L. Williams admitted this on the stand. He admitted that because Tom Miller had decided that Patsy had written the letter, he had to be taken down. He also admitted that his boss, Ramsey lawyer Hal Haddon, had asked his old buddy, Dave Thomas, the county prosecutor who went after Tom Miller, for a favor. It was a shameful incident of legal circle-jerking that was exposed in court. You have to wonder a few things. First, how many other people have been silenced by these goons (who are now working with the DA's office!)? Why would innocent people need to pull a stunt like this? And did the Ramseys know about it? If they didn't, then they had to realize how bad it made them look. If they did, and legally they would have to have known, then they ordered it.

Finally, in 2002, the dents became large holes. That year, American television screens were full of the faces of kidnapping victims, whose names we still remember to this day: Danielle Van Dam, Samantha Runnion, and Elizabeth Smart (who was returned safely, thank the gods). And of all of those little girls who were murdered, not one of them even remotely resembled what happened to JonBenet. For years, Team Ramsey told us that JonBenet was killed by some pedophile killer, and we were forced to see what real pedophile killers do: they don't kill their victims inside the home, they don't redress their victims, and they dump their victims after killing them. Lin Wood, the Ramsey lawyer, had the unmitigated gall to co-opt the pain these families were in to push his clients' wild claim. Well, he didn't get away with it. Nancy Grace, the tough-as-nails Southern hellcat prosecutor was on that Larry King show that night, as was Marc Klaas, who has been a tireless advocate for laws to protect children from predators ever since his daughter Polly was kidnapped from her bedroom and murdered by a career criminal who had just gotten paroled for the umpteenth time in 1993. And they didn't go for it. Nancy pointed out how different JonBenet's killing was from those other cases, and Klaas, who is in a unique position to understand just what an insult Wood was committing to the memories of the victims' families, really went to town, reminding the audience that, like the Ramseys claim they have, David Westerfield, the killer of little Danielle Van Dam, also had no history of violent or deviant behavior. He also noted the tendency the Ramseys and Wood have for threatening lawsuits against anyone who questions their version of what happened. And it was in that moment that I saw just what kind of people the Ramseys associate themselves with to destroy their enemies. Wood, this backwoods John Edwards-with-a-mean-streak redneck lawyer, sat there with his trademark "don't-fuck-with-me-punk" grin and said that no one should be intimidated by the facts, and if you don't know about the case, don't talk about it. The heated sibilance in his voice made his polite words poisonous with very thinly-veiled threats. I couldn't believe it. This man, supposedly an advocate for his "victim" clients, had just threatened a genuine victim's advocate. What's worse, Internet "sleuths" who genuflected every time John or Patsy Ramsey so much as sneezed (similar to what the media does with President Barack Obama), were absolutely butchering the Van Dam family in the same way they claimed the Ramseys were being attacked (which was nowhere near as vicious). It didn't help the cause that on that night, I caught a rerun of the Comedy Central Show "South Park." In it, the Ramseys are ruthlessly parodied (along with OJ Simpson) and told to "stop acting like victims and confess, you goddamn murdering murderers!"

By August of 2002, I was clearly in the camp of the people who say the Ramseys were involved. I had seen them for what they really were. The masks had fallen away, and the true faces were horrible to see. My father used to tell me, "always keep an open mind, just not so open that your brain falls out."

By chance, I discovered a web site that guided me to other sites where crime cases are discussed. JonBenet is a popular one to talk about. Among them are www.websleuths.com, www.crimenews2000.com, www.forumsforjustice.org, and others. To this day, you can find me at a few of them. There's actually a funny story behind that. Many of the people who post on the JonBenet forums, the ones who believe the Ramseys are involved in some way, have a strong affection for Detective Thomas. For a long time, they would ask me if I was him. I was sad to have to disillusion them.

The Internet subculture that surrounds this case is a fascinating phenomenon in and of itself. JonBenet's death was really the first "Internet-era" crime. In 1994, when OJ Simpson was first arrested, the Internet boom hadn't yet happened. JonBenet was right on the cusp of that. And, since the Simpson drama had just ended at the time, it was a great place to start. Today, these Internet forums, like the Roman Forum of old, are places where regular people can voice their feelings on certain issues, not just criminal ones. JonBenet is just the tip of the iceberg. Any high-profile case, along with some you've probably never heard of, can be found.

One of the original forum founders is a radio host from Utah named Tricia Griffith. She heads up www.forumsforjustice.org and www.websleuths.com. Another, on the other side of it, is Susan Bennett, a North Carolina housewife, more about her later. But it seems that the majority of "regulars" are actually women about Patsy's age: 35 and up. I don't really know why. Not all posters as those who participate are called are pleasant. Most, regardless of where you stand, are all right. But some are just plain no good. For that reason, moderators strictly enforce "Terms of Service." Although extremely rare, there have been instances of what has come to be known as "cyber-stalking." For those of you who don't know, this is where a person on the Internet will target a person they know or someone else on the Internet and subject them to harsh treatment, including, but not limited to, death threats. As of this writing, a poster identified only as "coloradokares" has been harassed repeatedly by a poster known only as "shill," and has actually gotten the local police involved. Whatever comes of it remains to be seen.

Darlene from Brandon, Florida, a poster at Websleuths.com writes:

> *The ransom note is one of the reasons I became suspicious of the Ramseys. It is so ridiculous and over-dramatized, and of course we know who had a penchant for drama. A kidnapper would have their plan all laid out in order to make entry, grab their victim and escape. They would have a note already prepared, short and concise as to request for ransom, and directives to JonBenet's parents. No kidnapper would hang around long enough to write a 3 page ransom note–not counting the practice pages in the waste basket. How would the kidnapper know where to find the notepad and the felt pen used to write the note, written on Patsy's notepad, with her pen? I believe the Ramseys planned to bring the body somewhere outside of the house, but feared they could be seen by someone. The ransom note was written to make LE think there really was a kidnapping........but it really was an attempt to cover up the murder of an innocent child.*

Another poster, who uses the screen name angelwngs, adds that, from her experiences as a kindergarten teacher, not every child who experiences sexual molestation will tell someone. According to this poster, one little girl confessed that she had grown to "like" it. That got me to thinking. So I dug around in some old crime encyclopaedias and found a case where a girl's father started molesting her around six-years-old and it continued until she was a teenager. It continued because she grew to enjoy it. After all, it was her father's idea of "quality time," and there's no bond stronger than between father and daughter. Just food for thought.

Other sites serve as information archives. You can find interview transcripts, handwriting samples, photographs, statements, updates and the occasional humorous parody. These may include blabbieville.tripod.com, www.jonbenetramsey.pbwiki.com and www.acandyrose.com, which, for my money is the best all around.

While it may be said by some that these people are obsessed with something that doesn't necessarily affect them, it should be noted that there are a great number of highly intelligent people with great ideas on how to solve a particular crime. Some have, in fact, done just that. The most notable example was the Danielle Van Dam case where investigators saw someone online talking about the last time that poor girl had a haircut and they put it to use. Danielle's killer is now rotting in prison in California, right where he belongs.

CHAPTER SEVEN

Conspiracy of Cowards, Creeps and Crooks—How The Ramseys Beat the Rap and Who's to Blame

Now that we have established what I think happened, that is that Patsy Ramsey killed her daughter by accident and her husband helped cover it up, we have to ask "what went wrong?" How could they get away with it with all the evidence I have presented? This chapter will examine just that.

Part of the blame lies with the Boulder Police Department. They believed that JonBenet had been kidnapped, and as such did nothing to secure the crime scene. They let the family and family friends traipse all over the house, contaminating everything, losing track of people, and allowing John Ramsey and Fleet White to find the body. Once that happened, the case was heavily damaged. Every step of procedure was ignored or just forgotten. And when the guys in charge refused to accept the fact that they were in over their heads, it spiraled from there.

Let's take a look at the police officers involved:

- Det. Linda Arndt. She was one of the cops on the scene that morning. She did not herd the gathered people out, told John Ramsey to search the house a second time, and later said she "saw murder in John Ramsey's eyes."

- Det. Rick French. He failed to find JonBenet's body. If he had lifted the door peg, he might have. He has to live with that the rest of his life.
- Det. Steve Thomas. He was called in on the case three days later. He's probably the most famous of the group, since he wrote a book. Thomas is seen as a hero by many who think the Ramseys killed JonBenet, and as the ultimate villain by those who don't, who try to do to him what OJ's shysters did to Mark Fuhrman in that case: destroy him and try to paint all of the case investigators with that brush. Thomas did everything he could for JonBenet, to hear him tell it. And many people who knew him say that he was as tough and smart a cop as there ever was. If anything could be said against him, it's that he's a macho guy with a shoot-first attitude, a strong believer in the death penalty (as am I) and seems to have an affinity for the "blue wall of silence." He was not a homicide detective. This was his first murder case, and that's a tall enough order. Nothing could have prepared him for something like this. He conducted the April 1997 interview with Patsy. According to his book, he had almost broken her when one of the DA's envoys stepped in and called a break. Needless to say he was frustrated. Anyone would have been. That pretty much set the tone for his tenure on the case. Finally, after the 1998 interviews, he'd had enough (more on that later.) He turned in his

badge. On August 6th, 1998, JonBenet's birthday, he resigned, releasing a letter to the media saying that his conscience wouldn't let him participate in the miscarriage of justice that the DA's office was perpetrating. After that, he wrote his book, which led to the face-off with both Ramseys on *Larry King Live.*

Thomas's tale has a sting in it, though. Thanks to that confrontation on Larry King, he was sued for his trouble. He had to sell his house to pay the legal talent he amassed to fight the Ramseys, saying that he welcomed the chance to depose them in court where they couldn't take the Fifth Amendment and where he wouldn't have to prove anything beyond a reasonable doubt, as long as the majority of evidence was on his side. After two years of legal wrangling, he settled out of court, after promising he would fight to the bitter end. Pretty much tells you all you need. He moved out of the country afterwards, building houses, like Jimmy Carter. Two days after Patsy Ramsey died, Steve and his wife welcomed a baby girl into their family. When I heard that, I wondered if maybe Patsy had been reincarnated, but only as a joke. I don't know what they named her, but may they all be blessed.

- Detectives Tom Trujillo, Melissa Hickman, Jane Harmer and Ron Gosage round out the rest.
- Sergeant Tom Wickman was the evidence man and liaison between the police and Grand Jury. He was the *de facto* head of the case.
- Commander John Eller. A macho squad commander from Florida, it was under Eller's

watch that many of the most serious blunders were committed, many of them his own, including his refusal to be "hand-held" by other agencies.

- Chief Tom Koby. A perfect fit for Boulder: a hippy-dippy brotherly-love type. A milquetoast who let the DA and the Ramseys jerk him around, refused outside help and made no attempt to stand up to the DA's office.
- Chief Mark Beckner. He came in to replace Koby. To date, he is still chief. For all of his talk about wanting to charge the Ramseys, he shot down a proposal that might have cracked the case one way or another. The Boulder Police, in conjunction with the Georgia Bureau of Investigation, were going to "bug" the Ramseys' Atlanta home. The idea was that the cops would watch the house, wait until everyone was gone, then sneak in and plant the "bugs," electronic listening devices that, if used properly, can pick up incriminating conversations. The phone would also be tapped. As Ed MacDonald, the FBI agent who worked on the Lufthansa Airline heist (made famous in Martin Scorsese's *Goodfellas*) said, everyone gives themselves up over the phone. It's so easy to forget that it's a live wire, a wire that can hang you. If worse came to worse and someone came into the house during the operation (a Title 3 operation for you police buffs), they were to grab something and run to make it look like a robbery. The Georgia operatives were all set to go when Chief Beckner called it off. He was worried it might get out that

they were doing this and cause a scandal. Typical of this case, indecision turned out to be worse than a wrong decision. As MacDonald will tell you if you ask him, a well-placed bug can make all the difference in the world. Thomas simply forgot one of the key rules of law enforcement: if you want to keep a secret, don't tell the boss. Hell, I wouldn't be surprised if the Ramseys had the DA's office bugged!

- Robert Miller, Daniel Hoffman and Richard Baer. They were the "Dream Team" that Thomas refers to many times in his book. They were expert law enforcement agents whose job was to act as consultants for the Boulder Police Department in the wake of increasing tensions with the District Attorney's office. All were smart, tough prosecutors, which the DA and his staff were not. The hiring of this "Dream Team" was seen by many as an "FU" to the DA.

The DA's office in this case merits special attention. It probably tells you all you need to know about the DA's conduct in this case when you find out that their biggest supporters were and are the prime suspects, the prime suspects' lawyers and a whole mess of scumbag defense lawyers, including Larry Pozner, who believes that everyone is innocent until proven guilty and even then they're innocent, because every single cop is a fascist bulldog, and Alan Dershowitz, whose latest claim to fame is giving legal succor to those within the government who think it's okey-doky to torture people. Let's take a look at an exchange between him and Det. Thomas from *Larry King Live* in 2000:

DERSHOWITZ: A *prosecutor should bring a case only when on the basis of admissible evidence the case would be proved to satisfaction of a jury beyond a reasonable doubt. That's the constitutional standard. That's the standard we respect all through this country, and I think that* Mr. *Hunter was absolutely right in not bringing this country, and I think that* Mr. *Hunter was absolutely right in not bringing this case. I've looked at the Thompson book. It's full of speculation, theory, innuendo. He says his hypothesis is this. You know, that wouldn't even be a close case.*

First of all, it's Thomas. Alan continued:

I think that Alex Hunter is, although he's become criticized, I think he's a constitutional hero. He's a man who has made a decision to take the barbs and the slings, and there are going to be many, because it's much easier to bring the case. It would take no courage to bring the prosecution, and then if the jury acquitted, blame it on the jury. But it takes a lot of courage for a district attorney to bite the bullet and take the hard decision, and say there was a murder, maybe it's even likely certain people did it, but likely isn't enough.

THOMAS: *Well, let me make one comment.* Mr. *Dershowitz is with all due respect, a notorious criminal defense attorney. Where is a Vincent Bugliosi or a Rudy Giuliani sitting next to* Mr. *Hunter, these guys, who I consider hero prosecutors making that argument.*

Ben Thompson, a Boulder County politician running for office at that time, summed it up on the same program: "It's political, the reason that it hasn't been prosecuted. And we have a district attorney's office that is more political than it is a prosecutor's office. I'm sitting here listening to those two talk, or those three talk, and it's strange to me that Alex sounds more like a defense attorney than a prosecutor, and that's part of the problem. Let me say there is a cancer in our DA's office, and whenever anybody points it out, what happens is they attack whoever points it out instead of addressing the issue and trying to solve the problem."

Patsy Ramsey had unqualified praise for the DA, Alex Hunter:

> *"I like the fact that he's determined to find out who did this and he wasn't going to rubber stamp the police decision."*

Boy, that's just heartwarming. I talked about Alex Hunter earlier, but I only touched on him. Now you're going to hear the story full-bore.

Alex Hunter is a no-good, weak bastard. I really don't need to say anything more about him than that, but I will. Alex Hunter did not want this case. He had been in office for almost thirty years without having to do much of anything. He hadn't taken a murder case to trial in almost ten years, he'd never brought the death penalty against anyone, and if not for the fact that trying to get a real, tough-on-crime prosecutor in the DA's office in Boulder is like trying to raise the *Titanic* remains with tweezers, probably would not have been in office so long. But Boulder has a crime rate that anyone would wish for, so he was kind of like a star on top of a Christmas tree. Then this case came along. He was cruising toward an easy retirement. He set up a definition of beyond a reasonable doubt that no one could meet. It's supposed to be "beyond a reasonable doubt," not "beyond any doubt whatsoever and then some." Hunter had to eliminate unreasonable doubt, as well. It has been said, only half-jokingly, that Alex Hunter would need a DNA match, a videotape of the perp committing the crime and a signed confession just to cut a deal. He gave the Ramseys so much evidence that the FBI was aghast and said he was a fool, and suggested that the police file malfeasance charges. He was BUSINESS partners with the Ramseys, as I mentioned. A blue-collar ironworker in the projects wouldn't get that kind of consideration. And he was weak. The police wanted to arrest the Ramseys, let them stew in jail for a while, and see which one cracked first. That is a STANDARD ploy in cases like this. It helps to remember that in cases of domestic homicide, guilty verdicts are not usually won on forensic evidence, since the kind of evidence you would expect to find in a case, such as hairs, fibers, DNA, etc., is expected to be there, since it's usually the killer's own house. In cases of domestic homicide, and there are several state and federal prosecutors who will bear me out on this, you solve it the old-fashioned way: you arrest both parties, throw them in jail, and if necessary, give them each the third degree in separate rooms until one of them confesses. In 1990, Lisa Steinberg, the illegally adopted daughter of Joel Steinberg and Hedda Nusbaum, was found beaten to death in her New York apartment. With no other recourse, the NYPD arrested both parents and jailed them. Hedda Nusbaum cracked. She hired a lawyer (Barry Scheck, who worked for OJ Simpson and the Boulder Police) and testified against her husband in exchange for immunity from prosecution. Joel Steinberg went to prison. What happened with the Steinbergs is exactly what the Boulder police wanted to do with the Ramseys. The

"Dream Team" lawyers told them to do it, Chief Beckner suggested that they do it, but Hunter wouldn't do it. Too bad. I guess he figured it was too "police-state-ish" for his taste. Worse than that, the man undercut his own witnesses! Here's what I mean: when a linguistic analyst was brought in to examine the ransom letter, Hunter was completely in his corner, until the analyst declared that Patsy Ramsey wrote it. After that, Hunter lost interest and leaked information to the press and the agencies that used this man's services to sabotage his career. And it worked. As of 2004, this expert's washed up as far as analysis goes.

The worst part was not only did Hunter think like a defense attorney, he surrounded himself with people who were more like defense attorneys than prosecutors. One was Peter Hofstrom. As I mentioned earlier, he had a tendency to whine when things didn't go his way. He had spent some years as a prison guard at California's infamous San Quentin prison, which he thought gave him a special insight into the minds of police officers. They didn't see it that way. The Boulder cops thought of him as a guy who had spent so much time listening to criminals that he had become overly sympathetic towards them and subconsciously hostile towards police officers. Take Det. Thomas's first encounter with Hofstrom, for example. In *Perfect Murder, Perfect Town*, Schiller describes the event as taking place at University Hill in the early 1990s. The Hill had become known as a place where young punks would do all kinds of mischief, a lot of it serious. One night, a young woman was arrested. Even though she was much smaller than Det. Thomas, she took him on. She threw a punch that broke his nose. Two weeks later, after the girl was charged with assaulting an officer, the girl's mother asked him not to "ruin" her daughter's life. When Hofstrom found out, he said to Thomas, "you charged the girl with a felony."

"She broke my nose," Thomas replied.

"I want to drop this to a misdemeanor."

"I'm not looking to ruin anyone's life," Thomas said, "but she tagged me. There has to be some consequence for her actions."

"Look, I worked San Quentin," Hofstrom said. "I know what a felon is, and goddamn it, I respect those guys on death row. I had to feed some of them their last meals. You don't know what a goddamn felon is."

"Where I come from, you don't punch a cop," Thomas replied. "She should consider herself lucky she didn't get her ass kicked."

Hofstrom later did drop it to a misdemeanor. Need I say more? Yes, I think I should. Hofstrom was the one who went off his head and accused the police of trying to ransom JonBenet's body and told that to the Ramseys. He was also the one most responsible for giving them all the evidence they had when they asked for it. When Det. Thomas had his now legendary face-off with the Ramseys, he later said, quote: "I thought how different things might have been if the district attorney's office had not shared a shred of evidence, a single secret, test results or investigative conclusions with these people." Hofstrom gave the store away.

Trip DeMuth, before ANY evidence was in, decided that the Ramseys couldn't do it. Why? Because he couldn't do it. That kind of thinking has NO PLACE in LE offices. I can forgive the average person for that kind of naiveté, but he should KNOW better! Let me tell you a little more about him.

To hear him tell it, he was taken off the case because he didn't think the Ramseys were guilty. That way he gets to portray himself as this martyr-hero. In truth, he has only himself and his utter lack of professionalism to blame. I'll give you some examples. After leaving the DA's office, he went to work for the law firm of Michael Bynum, the man who convinced the Ramseys that they needed lawyers in the first place. Would that not constitute a conflict of interest? He commented on the case of Jason Midyette, saying that just because a ten-month-old was dead with 28 fractures, it doesn't mean murder. I KID YOU NOT! This man openly mocked the police presentation of evidence at the FBI meeting, and what got him booted was when his lack of professionalism upset Michael Kane so much that Kane went to Hunter and said, "it's him or me." Det. Thomas talks about these incidents at length. Schiller also talks about him, quote: "The detectives hated DeMuth. They felt he always talked down to them and that he didn't know the case." Trip has a thing about "witch hunts." He said the cops were on a witch hunt against the Ramseys, a witch hunt against the parents who beat that 10-month-old to death, and when Mary Lacy spent thousands of taxpayer dollars to bring back a crank because he confessed to the crime, he became afraid of a witch hunt against the DA. That sounds like a DEFENSE attorney talking, like he just stepped out of a Perry Mason episode, and not a very good one at that. None of the DA's staff had any real expertise with Grand Juries. Some of them had never even tried any murder cases. They were used to handling indigent non-whites with public defenders, not a former Miss West Virginia whose husband is loaded and whose lawyer owns half the state! Who can hire their own experts! How many of us could do that?

COME ON, HOW MANY!?

Which brings me to the last idiot-in-chief, Mary Lacy. This woman could fuck up a cup of coffee. She is the person responsible for the case being where it is today. Early on, one of the suspects in the murder was Bill McReynolds. He was known as "Santa Bill," because he dressed up like Santa Claus every Christmas to entertain children. John Ramsey had hired him to play Santa Claus for JonBenet. His wife Janet was a playwright. It didn't help that in the 1970s, she had written a play about a girl who is killed in her basement. The McReynolds's were cleared early on by the police, but the DA's office was convinced he was their best bet. Mary Lacy had wanted to go after "Santa" Bill McReynolds from day one. She was biased in the favor of the Ramseys because of their status. She has so much as said so. Lacy is known as a radical feminist who lets her belief in women's innocence cloud her reason. She demonstrated that in the University of Colorado case, where, back in 2001, a group of football players were accused of rape. Lacy was gung-ho to prosecute, even though it was clear that there was no case. It was Duke before Duke, where the three lacrosse players were hung out to dry by an overzealous, politically motivated prosecutor. Another incident came in 2006 when a ten-month-old boy named Jason Midyette was beaten to death and she wouldn't take any action because the grandfather owns half of Boulder's Pearl Street Mall. Journalist Frank Coffman describes Lacy as a feminist who is very pro-woman, to the point where it clouds her judgment, as I just showed you. She's also a mother and a career woman. Nothing wrong with that. I'm not one of these "a woman's place is in the home" type guys. I'm secure enough in my manhood to say that if a woman wants it all, she can have it. I just hope she can handle it and she doesn't lose perspective. Since Mrs. Lacy can't keep her own son out of trouble (he was busted for DUI), I'd say she has. I think that Mary Lacy saw Patsy, a wealthy, successful mother and identified with her. She saw this successful, lovely lady being grilled by a bunch of macho male cops and that was it. She actually chastised Tom Haney for being too tough on Patsy during the '98 interviews. WHAT?! Number one, Haney was using by-the-book techniques. Two, if you look at the tape, he's being perfectly calm! No threats, no intimidation. He's very calmly giving her a chance to explain the evidence. Patsy is the one cursing and jumping around and acting like she's got a scorpion in her panties! What was LACY watching?! Tom Haney is one of the finest homicide detectives in the entire Rocky Mountain area, if not the country. His record speaks for itself. And here's this assistant DA, who at that time I don't think had ever tried a murder case in her entire career, and to my knowledge still hasn't, telling him he was too tough for using absolutely STANDARD interrogation techniques that the greenest rookie on the beat would know! Haney's general feeling was, "who the hell does she think SHE is?" Later on, she had the unmitigated gall to tell the cops that because they were men, they couldn't understand a woman's mindset. ARE YOU KIDDING ME?! That may or may not be true, but it's a hell of a way to decide guilt or innocence! She makes her predecessor look like Rudy Giuliani.

Her major contribution to the case came after Patsy Ramsey's funeral, which she attended, in a shocking display of unprofessionalism. In August of 2006, Mary Lacy announced that an arrest had been made and a suspect was in custody. His name was John Mark Karr, a former schoolteacher from Georgia with a history of deviant pedophilic behavior. He had been in contact with Michael Tracy, a professor of journalism at the University of Colorado at Boulder. Tracey had spent the last year or so before cultivating this man's story. Karr had contacted him under the Internet name "Daxis," and claimed to be the real killer. He was found in Thailand, the capital of perversion, where he was trying to fulfill his horrible urges. When arrested, he made a series of confessions, but as the days went by, his story unraveled, and the case against him with it. By the time he was back in the US, his relatives had established he was nowhere near Boulder, his story had collapsed, and Mary Lacy was on the defensive. She shouldn't have been, because this should not have happened. Her conduct violated the most basic elements of procedure that a first-year law student would know. It was clear to many that she was a pro-Ramsey partisan and was trying to give them a gift. There should have been a recall election. She should have been forced to resign. The case should have been taken over by capable professionals. But none of that happened, because after ten years nobody gave a damn. Journalist Jeff Shapiro writes, "It's no secret that in 1997, when Lacy was a sex-assault prosecutor under then-DA Alex Hunter, she was furious when he did not appoint her to work on the case. Because Hunter and the police shied away from the intruder theory, many law enforcement officials often wonder if Lacy's attempts to prove them wrong are driven more by her personal feelings than by the actual pursuit of justice."

How did an utter moron like Mary Lacy ever get into the kind of position she's in? Well, in 2002, Lin Wood, the Ramseys' attorney, threatened to sue the police department if they didn't turn over the case to the DA's office, when he knew full well that Mary Lacy was sympathetic to his clients. What kind of sleazy backroom deal is THAT?! I've never even heard of such a thing: a suspect's lawyer deciding who can and cannot investigate a homicide case? I'm not a legal expert, so I don't know if that could be constituted obstruction of justice, or collusion, or not, but it damn well ought to be a disbarring offense. As far as I know, it may be legal, but it can't be ethical. Then, when she had the case, she made absolutely no attempt to even contact any of the original investigators, she brought in a whole new team consisting of people totally loyal to her point of view, including private investigators paid by the Ramseys, not to find the killer, but, as John admitted in his court deposition, to build a defense and keep him and Patsy out of jail. Alex Hunter was a lousy DA, but at least he'd hear all sides. Lacy refuses to even talk to people who think the Ramseys might have been involved. That kind of "investigation" may fly in places like the Soviet Union or Zimbabwe or North Korea, but this is America, and we're supposed to be better than that. Mary Lacy reminds me of that line from Paul Simon's song "The Boxer," the one about how the man hears what he wants to hear and disregards the rest. Former Grand Jury prosecutor Michael Kane has publicly questioned Lacy's knowledge of the case, saying that he isn't sure she's even read the case file.

Michael Kane was truly the only bright spot in this sea of murky vapor. As I said before, he was an outsider to the case brought in because he had experience with Grand Juries and history of winning cases. To hear him tell it, as he did in an interview in 2002, he had his work cut out for him. It didn't take him long to realize that the DA's office had called him in to do a job they really did not want him to do: get an indictment against the Ramseys. According to Kane, the entire DA's office was already welded to the intruder theory. He was just window-dressing. If Det. Thomas is public enemy number one to the pro-Ramsey people, Kane is definitely number two. Ramsey supporters have accused him of everything from having no objectivity and being "overzealous" (if Michael Kane can be considered overzealous, may the gods help us all), to outright lying and unethical behavior, to which he has responded, "if I were not a public figure, I would force them to prove it." Tom Haney knew him as well, saying what a fair-minded man he is.

Since I brought up Michael Tracey earlier, now is a good time to mention his role in screwing up this case. Tracey, a native of England, is your typical Boulder professor: a Michael Moore-type with nothing but contempt for Americans. He is the man behind a series of so-called documentaries that are so unbalanced, they approach the area of propaganda. Tracey's "documentaries" supposedly prove the Ramseys' innocence and seek to excoriate the "if-it-bleeds-it-leads" media culture of America that brought about the rush to judgment against them. Tracey's "documentaries," like those of Michael Moore, are loaded with outright lies and distortions, which are too numerous to list here, but their omissions are even more grievous. Professor Tracey targeted a man named John Gigax as a suspect in the murder, saying that he was in hiding. Internet sleuth Tricia Griffith found him in 30 seconds with a Google search. And Tracey did this while Karr was confessing. Tracey swore he was the real killer as well. None of the TV ads for his "documentaries" ever mention that the Ramseys were instrumental in getting them made at all. Wonder why that is?

As far as I'm concerned, Tracey is just like his colleague Ward Churchill: an arrogant, lying, no-good son-of-a-bitch. I'm sure the wife he cheated on with one of his grad students would agree (or so Chris Wolf tells it). That he is allowed to get away with his propaganda is shocking. Personally, I wouldn't give two cents for him and Churchill put together, but if I were forced to choose between one of them, say by having a gun held to my head, I'd have to take Churchill, because at least he never tried to make any money off of a little girl's murder. For Tracey to complain about the lack of ethics in today's media is the ultimate in hypocrisy, and the idea that he is teaching the next potential generation of journalists is a profoundly terrifying prospect, and the more people know about it, the better.

Another guy I reserve special contempt for is Lin Wood, the Atlanta litigation attorney who represents the Ramseys. Earlier I mentioned him, but the real picture is nothing short of disgusting. This guy took over as the Ramseys' lawyer in 2000, and made it his life's work to make sure everyone knew they were innocent, or else. To this end, he brings lawsuits or the threat of lawsuits against anyone who so much as suggests that the Ramseys aren't saints. Steve Thomas is only one of them. Thing is, he never takes any of them to court. Wood is a nuisance lawyer who finds out how much a party is insured for against lawsuits, and then settles for that amount. Whether he believes in their innocence or not, it certainly doesn't keep him from making the money, which he bragged about in court in 2002:

MR. WOOD: And it will be the
pleasure of my career when I take you down, and
that day may yet come because you still run
your mouth to the media so much that you're
going to get yourself sued eventually, you're

going to get your experts sued eventually, so
you just keep the business coming, Darnay. It's
really good for my pocketbook. I'm taking a

recess.
MR. HOFFMAN: *I know in this case*
that the Ramseys aren't paying a penny, the
insurance company is paying you finally, okay,
which is nice–
MR. WOOD: *Hey, I made more money*
handling the Ramsey case than you've made in
your whole damn career practicing law, Darnay.

I don't know about any of you, but that seems like the kind of thing you say to your fellow lawyers in a bar after hours, not in a court of law.

Wood is an ugly, confrontational bully who uses litigation to enrich his personal finances. He brags about the champion racehorses and custom Jaguar automobiles he buys with the proceeds. This practice is known as barratry. It's against the canons of ethics and is grounds for having a law license revoked. In 2006, Wood called former Boston prosecutor Wendy Murphy to threaten her as well. In her book, *And Justice For Some*, she talks about the experience:

> "I knew ahead of time that Wood was a thug because his reputation preceded him. The phone call only confirmed that reputation. 'Wendy Murphy,' he began with a bombastic twang, 'this is Lin Wood. I just heard you accuse my client of abusing and killing his daughter, and if I ever hear you say that again, you won't be ex-prosecutor Wendy Murphy, you'll be

> defendant Wendy Murphy in my lawsuit. Check my record.'"
>
> "In response to which I said, 'Check your record? Kiss my ass!' Then I told him he had a lot of nerve threatening me. It's interesting that it's okay for the Ramseys to discuss theories about innocent people being involved, but it's not okay for other people to discuss theories about the Ramseys' possible involvement."

She goes on to talk about how, for all of his highfalutin' rhetoric about principles and protecting his clients from the harsh opinions of others, Wood doesn't seem to mind dishing it out. When he represented the victim in the Kobe Bryant case, he was well aware that the stories about the victim having sex with three men in three days were damn lies, but he never tried to refute them, much less threaten anyone over them.

In 2003, Wood claimed to prove that the 911 call was a lie, that there were no voices heard at the end. He broadcast a tape on NBC that summer. Trouble is, it was an edited tape. Lawrence Schiller commented on this in July 2003, saying that Wood was editing facts to protect his clients, and that he was offended that Wood implied that he was a fool for reproducing an inaccurate transcript. The tape aired was a third-generation copy, not the enhanced original, and seemed to be partially erased, because the area which purports to show Burke's voice goes completely dead—no static, no breathing, nothing at all for four seconds. The sound comes back right before the final hang-up. Pretty sloppy, Wood.

He ought to pat himself on the back. Yes, folks, you too can get rich being a slimy, ugly, bald, unprincipled maggot with a law degree. All it will cost you is your soul. Wood is a bully, and bullies have to be stood up to. I'm glad Wendy Murphy stood firm. If more people did like she did, people like Wood wouldn't be able to do their evil work. Lin Wood is a major reason why this case went nowhere. He bullied a DA's office into protecting child-killers. I hope he has a damn good story when he stands before the judgment. He'll need it. As far as I'm concerned, Lin Wood, you slimy, ugly, bald unprincipled maggot son-of-a-bitch, you can kiss my ass!

John Douglas is the top FBI profiler in the world, at least to hear him tell it. Just ask him. The Ramseys hired him in January 1997 to do a profile of a possible killer. After spending only four hours with John Ramsey, during which time he did not even talk to Patsy Ramsey, he proclaimed the Ramseys innocent. He has never backed down from that opinion, even though many of his colleagues have very rightly trashed him for denying his own teachings to give them a pass. One of them is Gregg McCrary; a man who Douglas claims is one of the best. He was asked by the Ramseys as well, but turned them down because that's not the proper procedure. Another is Brent Turvey. In his book, *Criminal Profiling,* he had this to say:

> "First, Douglas was not given access to the police reports, the physical evidence, the crime-scene photos, the autopsy report, or the autopsy photos. The basis for any insight into offender behavior with the victim was elicited from the 4 1/2 hour interview conducted by Douglas with the parents, and their recollection. This breaks many of the rules of criminal profiling, which include his own, regarding the need for reliance on physical evidence and access to adequate input.

"Second, Douglas broke an inviolable rule of suspect interview strategy. He interviewed the parents together, as opposed to separately. As any interviewer will explain, it is important to interview suspects separately, not jointly, for any evaluations, and subsequent profiling work, to be valid. Conducting independent interviews of suspects allows the investigator to compare responses for inconsistencies and determine the veracity of each suspect's responses. Douglas did not do this.

"And finally, Douglas went on national television and endorsed the innocence of his client based upon this poorly rendered, almost boilerplate profile. This breaks the most important ethical rule of criminal profiling, which is that criminal profiles alone should not be used to address the issue of guilt. And even if they were, what Douglas feels in his heart about a case is not relevant. What is important is what the facts of the case suggest, behaviorally. As Douglas did not have the facts of the case at his disposal, it is the opinion of this author that he had no business rendering any opinions on the case whatsoever."

Robert Ressler, the founder of the Behavioral Sciences Unit, also criticized Douglas in a radio interview. He didn't name him, but anyone who followed the case would know who he meant.

Douglas's ego is clearly out of control, made obvious by every interview he gives concerning the case. He advised the Boulder police to work with the FBI, and then became angry when the FBI disagreed with him. One even said, "if the Ramseys aren't guilty, I'll turn in my credentials." He denies his own writings about staging to say that the scene wasn't staged, and seems to bear Det. Thomas a special grudge for having the temerity to point out how Douglas sold himself out like the worst whore in the street. I personally would consider it a badge of honor to be hated by this guy. He doesn't mention the other profilers, such as Turvey, McCrary, Ressler and Ron Walker, who go against him, though. I guess he figures it's easier to target a narcotics cop than to match wits with his fellows, who might actually know something about the profession.. Now he claims he took no money and never did any profile. He sure has a bad memory for a lawman. That he was allowed to speak before the Grand Jury pretty much tells you how committed the DA's office was to getting justice for JonBenet.

One who tried to testify is Susan Bennett. A North Carolina housewife who claims to have seen a vision in the shower proving the Ramseys to be innocent, she started her own online forum, with new members expected to pay her fifty dollars to join. Over the years, she has consistently tried to involve herself in the case. Her biggest coup involved Vassar professor Donald Foster, the man who I mentioned was sabotaged by Alex Hunter.. Foster, who claimed to be a linguistic detective, was contacted by the DA's office in 1997 and asked to analyze the ransom letter. When he concluded that Patsy Ramsey wrote the note, Alex Hunter and "Trip" DeMuth did their best to undercut him. That's where Bennett comes in. Under the name "jameson," she received notice from Foster, before he had a chance to review the actual case, that he had nailed her as the killer, claiming that she was actually John Andrew Ramsey. Foster then sent Patsy Ramsey a letter saying that he believed her to be innocent. That letter would come back to haunt him. But Bennett did not stop there. Working with Det. Lou Smit, Bennett serves as an Internet attack dog in the vein of Lin Wood, insulting anyone who does not agree with her as "BORG." This epithet is an acronym, meaning "Bent On Ramsey Guilt." It also recalls the Borg from *Star Trek*, a race of mechanically-enhanced people who share a collective consciousness, the implication being that none of the people who think the Ramseys guilty are capable of independent thought. That a loose cannon like this would be allowed near the case at all, much less to work with an actual detective is a damn good indication of the lack of integrity endemic to the case. Earlier, when I mentioned how unpleasant certain Internet sleuths can be, Bennett was foremost in my mind. Well, turnabout is fair play. Det. Thomas, in his inimitable style, summed her up well: a code-six wing nut. Apparently, if his deposition is to be believed, John Ramsey felt the same way, at least at first. In 2002, the Ramseys found out that Bennett had been selling case information to tabloid magazines. Their relationship suffered, as you can imagine. On a personal level, she insulted me, your humble author as well. Consider this the receipt.

Steve Ainsworth was another one deserving of mention. He was an investigator from the Boulder County Sheriff's Department. Sadly, he was blinded by the Smit aura and judged the Ramseys innocent without ever reading the full case-file. He attacked his fellow cops in a shocking display of unprofessionalism and did a break-dance to make the evidence fit an intruder, believing that the intruder staged the crime scene so it looked like the Ramseys had staged the crime scene to look like an intruder. Confused yet? Yeah, so am I. Confused how he wasn't booted the first week.

In 1998, the District Attorney called a Grand Jury to look into the case. Grand Juries are investigative bodies who can issue indictments against suspects if sufficient probable cause exists. Since the standard is so low, it has become common knowledge that a good prosecutor can get a Grand Jury to indict a ham sandwich. As Det. Thomas remarks in his book, it was clear the sandwich was in no danger. The adage overlooks another reality: a ham sandwich doesn't have million-dollar lawyers. The guys in charge of empaneling the Grand Jury were "Trip" DeMuth, Pete Hofstrom and Lou Smit. Any questions? Considering that no one in the DA's office wanted to convene a Grand Jury in the first place and felt forced to do so in the wake of Steve Thomas's resignation, lest the Governor step in, is it any wonder it went nowhere? What's more, none of the actual detectives who worked the case were called to testify. Why do it at all? Burke Ramsey was called, but not John and not Patsy. They were never grilled by the prosecutors and shown to the Grand Jury for what they were. What the hell were these people doing?

People like to point to the fact that the Grand Jury didn't indict as evidence that the Ramseys are innocent. But there's actually no real proof that they didn't vote to indict. The decision is ultimately up to the DA. He can crush an indictment and thanks to Grand Jury secrecy laws, doesn't have to let on. In 2006, Barry Scheck said that it was Hunter who decided not to indict. From what Henry Lee has said, he convinced Hunter not to go forward.

As Det. Thomas mentioned in his book:

- the grand jury might have the sole mission of helping secure records, testimony, and evidence.
- it might not hear the entire case at all.

- it would not be used to obtain an indictment
- and if a runaway grand jury somehow returned an indictment of its own, the DA would not be obligated to prosecute.

Also, it didn't help that the Grand Jury would only meet for a few days every month or so. How were they supposed to retain anything?

In 2006, a grand Juror went public, offering more insight into the workings of the Grand Jury. This juror, who shall remain nameless since she is not a public figure, said that when the coroner made his presentation and the autopsy photos were viewed, none of the Grand Jurors could believe that a mother could do that to her child. She seemed to suggest that as a mother herself, she went into the proceedings feeling that way.

As always, I'm struck by how naive people can be. I guess they didn't talk to Ron Walker, the FBI man on the scene that morning. He was interviewed by the cable channel "A&E." When asked straight out if a parent were capable of doing what was done to JonBenet, he was forced to say yes. Here's what he had to say:

> *"Well, as much as it pains me to say it, yes, I've seen parents who have decapitated their children, I've seen cases where parents have drowned their children in bathtubs, I've seen cases where parents have strangled their children, have placed them in paper bags and smothered them, have strapped them in car seats and driven them into a body of water, any way that you can think of that a person can kill another person, almost all those ways are also ways that parents can kill their children."*

However, in October of 2013, it was finally made public that the Grand Jury in the case did in fact issue an indictment against both parents for "child abuse resulting in death." Alex Hunter misled the country into thinking that there had been no indictments. The truth will out.

And last, but certainly not least is the law firm of Hal Haddon, Bryan Morgan and Lee Foreman, the defense attorneys that John Ramsey hired to represent him. I mentioned some of their more underhanded dealings earlier, such as the incident with Tom Miller. But that is only one indication of their any-dirty-trick-necessary approach to defending clients. It is often said, including by those in all areas of the legal profession that a defense attorney's duty is to their client, not the truth. This is more-or-less codified in their part of the legal canons: even if they have knowledge that their client is guilty, they still have to provide the best possible defense that they can give, and if they don't, they will face punishments up to and including having their law licenses revoked.

What separates Haddon and his collaborators apart from the general pack of wolves is that most defense attorneys at least care a little bit about whether or not their client is innocent. Haddon doesn't seem to mind that one iota. Those who have visited his office in Colorado have seen a plaque bearing the firm's motto:

Reasonable Doubt for a Reasonable Fee

They don't CARE! As long as you have the cash to afford their services, Haddon and his wrecking crew will go to the mat for you, using any slimy, underhanded tactic that is available to them. And their prices must be reasonable indeed, since theirs is the only law office I'm aware of that features an Olympic-size swimming pool! This is what John Ramsey bought with his money: a powerful, politically well-connected group of sharks who sell themselves like the worst whores in the street. And I truly believe that any self-respecting prostitute would take that as an insult.

There are two more goofs in this mess who should be mentioned, but they deserve special mention.

CHAPTER EIGHT

The Fox Chases His Own Tail

In March of 1997, the DA contacted Andrew Louis Smit, known as Lou.

A retired detective with an office in Colorado Springs, he had made a rep in Amarillo, Texas as a homicide man. He had a record for solving homicides. He possessed an easygoing, aw-shucks manner that, to hear his friends tell it, masked a human bloodhound. Most of the people who knew him and know him consider him their friend. This made him seem like the right man to lead the case and teach the inexperienced Boulder Police a thing or two.

That's not what happened. Three days after arriving on the case, before he'd even read the file, he sat back in his chair and said, "I don't think the Ramseys did it." He never budged from that position.

Another incident which took place later set it in concrete. Smit, a devout Christian (the kind who picket abortion clinics), had been approached by the Ramseys to pray with them. Knowing that this tactic had won confessions in the past, he agreed. He came out of that meeting a believer in them.

That SHOULD have been the deal-breaker right there. Any good attorney would tear him apart for even the

APPEARANCE of impropriety. But he was allowed to remain for another year-and-a-half. The intruder theory owes its existence to him. Smit is often referred to as the evidence man in the case. He puts so much stock in evidence, he makes up his own! This would be a good time to list the so-called evidence of the intruder and take it on, and him in the bargain.

- Smit believes that the intruder entered and exited the house through the window in the basement, using the suitcase to climb out again. Earlier, I showed you how that couldn't have happened. But perhaps I didn't mention how the grate that the intruder supposedly lifted and replaced had an intact spider-web attached to it and the well. Dr. Brent Opell identified it as the web of the agelendae species, saying that they hibernate during the winter and could not have respun a web in that time. Moreover, the Ramseys had an alarm system and a dog. Neither was a factor, but how would a stranger know that? In an interview with Smit in 1998, John Ramsey said that when he broke the window in the summer of 1996, he climbed down into the window well, turned his back, knelt down and slid in:

  LOU SMIT: So you say you just went down into the window well where you kicked out the window. Then what did you have to do? What's your next step?

  JOHN RAMSEY: Then you had to reach in to unlatch the window, and if it's stuck, you just pop it open. I mean, I don't remember if I slid in face forward or a turned around. Probably turned around, turn around backwards and put your knees on the ledge here and let your feet in and then just drop down. That's probably how I would have done it.

But as Smit later proved himself, the window well just isn't wide enough to do all of that. Plus, John would have had to drop a considerable distance on his hands and knees. Not only that, but it's helpful to remember that it's not as easy as all that to just slide in because the window doesn't open all of the way. It only opens about halfway because of an overhanging pipe. Not only that, but there's doubt about his story. He forgot his key, found himself locked out and broke a window, took off his clothes and slid in? Wouldn't it have been easier to get a spare key from the neighbor across the street? Or break a pane on the door a short distance away, reach in, unlock it and get in that way? Something doesn't wash. For my money, the police would not have bothered questioning John about the window unless they already knew that it had been broken the night of the murder, but that's just my gut talking.

He believes that the intruder entered the house after the Ramseys left and made himself at home. It's a large, rambling house, easy to hide in. Yet, we are supposed to believe that a stranger could navigate the entire house in the dark and memorize its layout in just a few hours when the housekeeper who had been there three days a week for a year got lost. We're supposed to believe that he did all this without leaving a trace of himself. Locard's theory holds that all contact leaves some evidence.

- Smit believes that the killer spent that time writing the ransom letter, and the practice note before that. He bases his belief on the idea that no one, not even a psychopath could be calm enough to write it after the killing. Smit is echoing the sentiments of John Douglas on this one. Smit, showing his true colors, is supposed to have told Douglas, "it took me eighteen months to figure out the Ramseys were innocent. It took you four days." Get a room, you guys. Oddly, Smit was at the FBI meeting, where the profilers, who have much more experience dealing with psychopaths than Smit has, told them that the note was written afterwards and indicated the writer was not calm. Smit could have said something to them. He said exactly nothing.
- Smit believes that the ransom letter's "violent language" excludes the Ramseys, saying that they weren't the type of people to write such things as "she dies, she dies, she dies." Smit is fooling himself. Many profilers and linguistic analysts have examined the note and found it to be very passively voiced and full of maternal instructions. Besides, if writing violent stuff makes one a killer, I'm sure Mr. Smit would like to lock up Quentin Tarantino and Eli Roth!
- When asked why the killer didn't bring a note with him, he says that the killer didn't want to get caught with it on him in case he got stopped

by the cops. Apparently, he finds that easier to believe than the more obvious answer. Quite frankly, if he had gotten caught, all he had to do was give them some story. He could have told them it was a joke. Anyone reading that note would have agreed with him.

- Then, there's the kind of killer Smit thinks did this. He thinks it was a pedophile. He describes JonBenet as a "pedophile's dream." The idea that a pedophile killer would attack JonBenet with a paint brush rather than feel her himself is pretty out there, but I guess Smit was absent that day when the FBI explained that pedophile kidnappers don't leave ransom notes. It's simple motive: one is motivated by lust, the other by greed. It would be the first time there was a crossover.

  More importantly, pedophiles are incurable. They keep striking until they get caught or die. The FBI had never seen a case like this. More importantly, to this day, they've never seen another one either. Not one single girl has been found bashed, strangled and violated with an object with a note left at the scene. There's only one, and JonBenet is it.

- Smit believes that the killer used a stun gun to subdue JonBenet. Since the Ramseys didn't have one, that lets them out, to his way of thinking. For those of you who don't know, a stun gun is a non-lethal self-defense weapon that uses an electrical charge to bring down an attacker. It's thought of as more effective than pepper spray.

> It works by focusing a low-wattage, high-voltage charge into a person's body causing their muscles to overwork and shut down. In this way, it leaves no permanent damage. Smit thinks it knocked JonBenet out long enough to take her from her bed. This is the most notable instance of several where Smit just made up evidence out of whole cloth. Firstly, as someone who owns a stun gun, I can tell you it does not render a person unconscious. It's not made for it. It's also a highly impractical weapon for this kind of crime, because it makes a lot of noise and causes the person to scream when zapped.

Here's where it falls apart. The prongs on the Air Taser stun gun are rectangular and spaced 3.5 cm from inside to inside. The marks on JonBenet's body are only 2.9 cm apart. One of the "prong" marks is not even properly aligned. By that, I mean provided you could get a subject to hold still long enough to put only two marks on them, as Smit did with the sedated pig, they would run parallel to each other in every respect. One of the marks is tilted to the left.

Smit failed to listen to the forensic pathologists who discussed the stun gun. One of them was Dr. Werner Spitz. In 2002, Spitz agreed with the autopsy report, which described these marks as scratches (abrasions), not burns. Instead, Smit shopped experts until he found one who agreed with him. First he contacted Robert Stratbucker, who is generally acknowledged as the leading authority on stun guns. Stratbucker said in 2001 that he wrote back to Smit telling him that he was wrong. "I guess that wasn't what he wanted to hear," Stratbucker commented, "because I never heard from him again." Finally, Smit came across Arapaho County coroner Michael Doberson, who can be relied on to agree with anything Smit says. Doberson agreed with him, saying, "My experiments, and the observations that we made and all the work that's been done, I feel that I can testify to a reasonably degree of medical certainty that these are stun gun injuries."

Trouble is, he'd already said he couldn't agree: "You really can't tell from a photo," Doberson said in 1998.

Doberson's expertise stems from a case where a stun gun was used. Gerald Boggs was murdered in the area. The body of Gerald Boggs was exhumed after it had been buried for 8 months by the infamous Dr. Doberson. It was then proven that a stun gun was used on him which helped convict his ex-wife and her lover of Boggs' murder. A stun gun which matched the marks just below Boggs' ear was found in his ex-wife's car. The problem was, the photos of the marks taken after he was exhumed don't match the marks on him when he was fresh: The fresh marks are bright red and erratic, just like they were on me when I was zapped. Doberson can't even tell the real thing.

In 2001, Smit and Doberson stun gunned some pigs to try and reproduce the marks on JonBenet. They couldn't do it. They always got bright pink marks, not the dirty brownish ones on JonBenet. Worse, Smit claimed that the blue line between the marks on JonBenet's body were caused by the bluish electrical arc between the prongs. Not only is this laughable, he couldn't even reproduce the blue mark on the pigs. It should be noted that the pigs were highly sedated when zapped, not fighting like someone alive would be. JonBenet's body should have looked like Boggs: like a fire-ant attack.

Steven Tuttle, an executive for Air Taser, said this: "We have never seen those types of marks when you touch somebody with a stun gun," he said. "We are talking hundreds of people that have been touched with these devices. I can't replicate those marks." He also said the Air Taser does not render people unconscious and zapped himself on camera to prove it. In 2006, Tom Wickman was interviewed, saying that they had eliminated the possibility of a stun gun. In 2002, Werner Spitz went public on his findings on the marks, saying that they were most likely caused by a snap on an article of clothing. When he says a snap, he means those little metal buttons.

Perhaps Patsy Ramsey herself can shed some light on the subject:

TOM HANEY: Okay. Anything else on the bed?

PATSY RAMSEY: Well, this looks like a little —the little pot holder square she was making. This multicolored thing here. This black thing I can't (INAUDIBLE). Oh, that's sort of looks like it might be the little velvet dress (INAUDIBLE). <u>Little silver snaps.</u>

TRIP DeMUTH: When did she last wear that?

PATSY RAMSEY: She wore that to the Whites on the 25th.

TRIP DeMUTH: Okay. The evening of the 25th?

Shockingly, this instance of creating evidence that does not exist is not the worst breach of ethics committed by Smit.

- Smit asserts that fibers not matched to anything in the house were found in the basement. Never mind that no one can say how long they were there or whether they matched the items taken out of the house by Patsy Ramsey's sister Pamela. Never even entered his mind, I guess.

- Smit contends JonBenet ate pineapple from a Tupperware container that the killer brought with him. Sure, he brings a cumbersome pineapple dish, but no note?
- Smit claims that the knots in the cord used to strangle JonBenet were highly sophisticated knots and that no one in the Ramsey family could have tied them. Again, he whips something out of thin air, First of all, John Ramsey was an accomplished sailing enthusiast. He would know how to tie a knot. But it doesn't matter. The knots were not sophisticated. Anyone could have tied them. In 2003, Michael Kane mentioned them on MSNBC:

> *"I don't know where this came from that these were sophisticated knots. I don't know that anybody had the opportunity to untie those knots who was an expert in knots, but the police department had somebody who fit that category and that was not the opinion of that person. These were very simple knots."*

Kane mentioned a knot expert hired by the Boulder police. He doesn't name him, but he was most likely John Van Tassel from the Royal Canadian Mounted Police, who is mentioned in Det. Thomas's book.

- Smit believes that the head blow came last, since JonBenet did not bleed heavily into the skull. This is contradicted by several pathologists, including Werner Spitz, Thomas Henry, Henry Lee, and Ronald Wright. In his book, Schiller says that they agreed the head wound could have been anywhere from ten to forty-five minutes before the strangulation. "She was whopped on the head a long time before she was strangled," said Wright in an interview for the *Rocky Mountain News*. 'That might or might not have rendered her unconscious. But this is not anything that kills her right away.' He said 20 to 60 minutes elapsed between the skull fracture and the strangulation.

The blood story is another fantasy. The autopsy report describes three different areas of bleeding: the scalp hemorrhage, the subdural hematoma, and a subarachnoid hemorrhage. What's more, the sulci and the gyri were flattened against the skull. That means JonBenet's brain swelled so much it was pressed against the inside of her skull. That takes time. What's more, according to Denver neurologist Kerry Brega, it's fairly common for head wounds not to bleed. "We see a lot of people with skull fractures without bleeds in the brain, and they didn't all get strangled on the way in," she said.

This leads into another story. Smit claims that since JonBenet's head wound came last, she must have fought her killer while being strangled. He describes multiple scratches on JonBenet's neck where she clawed at the rope. He can't even keep his own story straight. First he says she was stun gunned to keep from fighting, then she fought like a hellcat. Trouble is, the autopsy photos clearly show no signs of any kind of scratches: The autopsy report describes no scratches, only petechial hemorrhages. The Fox is chasing his tail again. To better explain this, Websleuths.com poster AMES has a unique perspective on the subject of strangulation. As a young girl, she was strangled. She survived with no known permanent physical damage, but she has never forgotten:

> *I would just like to say that when I was really young, and in Elementary School, I rode the bus with a high school boy, that I swear was Satan's son. He was really mean to all of the younger kids on the bus. While I was sitting in one of the seats, minding my OWN business, he was sitting directly behind me. He took a cord, about the width of a shoestring, and placed it in front of my neck, and began to pull as hard as he could, from behind. As he was doing this, I heard his grunts....from pulling so tight...and in between his grunts, his laughter. He apparently thought this was funny!! Anyway, I can still remember gasping for air, as my throat closed in...and also scratching my neck, trying desperately to remove the cord so that I could breathe. As I was about to lose consciousness....Satan's son finally let go. I will never forget that feeling as long as I live. Having your airway cut off, is a terrible feeling. I almost clawed my neck to shreds...just trying to get my fingers under it enough so that I could at least TRY to pull it away. My strength, being an elementary student, was no match for the male*

(Satan's son) high school student. He was suspended from the BUS! Geez....what a "high" price to pay, for "merely" trying to strangle someone. His butt should have gone to juvenile detention. I was not the only person that he did this to, this guy was a "real sweetheart". His name is Andrew Miller. His whole family is a bunch of idiots and jailbirds. He has several brothers and sisters, and they are ALL CRAZY!! This is unrelated to the JonBenet case, but...for no reason but jealousy...his sisters jumped on my sister, and pulled out several grocery BAGS full of hair. It happened on the school bus, and the bus driver had to sweep it all up. We had to get a restraining order against THEM too. Now for the reason that I have went into my memory bank, and pulled this out....I believe that JonBenet's head injury came first, and then the strangulation....or ELSE...she would have had severe scratches on her neck, from trying to remove the cord, AND would have had lots of her own FRESH skin (not old DNA that is always present) under her fingernails. In my opinion the head wound came first...followed by the strangulation. Trust me....I should know.

- Smit talks about a hand print left on the basement door, a footprint from a Hi-Tec shoe and a pubic hair on the blanket JonBenet was wrapped in. In 2002, it was revealed that the police had traced those items down. The palm print was matched to Melinda Ramsey, with a videotape to prove it. Thanks to the Grand Jury testimony of Fleet White and his son, Fleet III, it was found out that

Burke Ramsey owned a pair of Hi-Tec shoes. His parents even described them as having a compass in them. Lastly, through mitochondrial DNA testing, the hair was determined to have come from Patsy Ramsey, and it was actually an arm hair.

Smit has always claimed that if evidence were to arise implicating the Ramseys, he'd go after them. But on several occasions, that has happened. and he was one of the first to pooh-pooh it. In 2000, Gideon Epstein, one of the country's leading handwriting experts, studied the ransom letter, then offered to have Smit go over his findings with him. Smit flat-out refused. Why? If he's the man he says he is, he certainly wouldn't turn down a good lead, right? And if Epstein's conclusions are nothing but hooey, if Smit's evidence of innocence is so overwhelming, what could he possibly have to fear? Secondly, he claimed that the fibers that actually can be traced to the night of the killing, those from Patsy Ramsey, don't mean anything. Although when pressed, he conceded that they are incriminating. Smit apparently thinks he's smarter than all the experts, Epstein being just one example. During his deposition in a lawsuit filed against the Ramseys (more on that later), he essentially admitted that he didn't speak to anyone who didn't agree with him:

A. *Because I think he came to the wrong conclusion.*

Q. *But can't an expert that is well qualified reach the wrong conclusion occasionally?*

> *MR. WOOD: Are you asking him to comment on Dr. Spitz's qualifications?*
>
> *MR. HOFFMAN: Well, yeah, I asked him why he didn't feel he was qualified, and he said just because he came to the wrong conclusion. That doesn't necessarily mean he is not qualified.*
>
> *MR. WOOD: All I am saying is to the form of your question, your question assumes a well-qualified expert.*
>
> *MR. HOFFMAN: Okay. Then I am going to ask –*
>
> *Q. (By Mr. Hoffman)—Detective Smit whether you think Werner Spitz is a well-qualified expert?*
>
> *A. Personally, no.*
>
> *Q. Okay. And the reasons for that?*
>
> *A. Mainly because I have seen his reports. I have also talked to other doctors and pathologists. They do not agree with Warner Spitz. I will also go by what they say.*

As dedicated as he claims to be, you might think he'd take a minute to talk to Werner Spitz first!

Smit thinks he knows more than Dr. Richard Krugman, as well:

> *Q. But Dr. Richard Krugman is the dean of the, I think, Colorado University Health Sciences Center, and is considered a nationally-known child abuse expert, and apparently doesn't agree with you.*

MR. WOOD: *Are you talking about, when you say "sexually molested," are you representing that Dr. Krugman is taking the position that there was not a sexual assault as evidenced by the trauma to JonBenet Ramsey's vagina?*

MR. HOFFMAN: *No. That simply that there wasn't sexual gratification as a motivation behind it; that there was some sort of an assault on the sex organs, but they weren't necessarily for the purposes of sexual gratification. That is the representation.*

MR. WOOD: *So the representation is that Dr. Krugman acknowledges that she was physically assaulted with some type of instrument in her vaginal area, but Dr. Krugman, you represent, has some theory as to why that attack took place that would differ from –*

MR. HOFFMAN: *No, I just want you –*

MR. WOOD: *Excuse me.*

—the idea that it was a sexual motivation?

MR. HOFFMAN: *I just wanted to ask Detective Smit whether or not he had heard that and whether he knew of it.*

MR. WOOD: *I am just not sure what he is being asked to say that he heard of.*

Q.*(By Mr. Hoffman) Simply —well, have you heard that Dr. Krugman does not believe that this was a sexual assault involving gratification?*

A. *No, I have not.*

Again, would it be asking too much to talk to him?!

Talk is cheap. If it comes from Lou Smit, it's even cheaper.

- Finally, Smit's big claim is the DNA. JonBenet had DNA not from a family member under her nails, in her underwear and on the waistband of her leggings. This leads him and Mary Lacy to think that JonBenet fought her killer, scratched him, he pulled down her pants, drooled into the panties, and molested and killed her. Trouble is, none of the DNA was fresh. It was in a state referred to as "degraded." It was old DNA. They had to use a replication method just to identify enough alleles to say that it was human. Forensic scientist Henry Lee said that JonBenet's murder will not be solved by DNA alone. What us lay people have to remember is that DNA is everywhere. We all have some on us. The advancing DNA technology is a double-edged sword. The more sensitive it gets, the more likely it is to pick up DNA that is not relevant to the crime scene. Yes, it may be DNA from a person outside the family, but the tests don't say how or when it got there. The DNA under her nails only had three markers, nowhere near enough to say if it even matches the DNA elsewhere. Their imaginations give it power. Ian Rodway, chief deputy attorney for the Commonwealth of Virginia, said DNA evidence could be very useful when given the right context. 'That's not to say it doesn't have its limits. Finding traces of a person's DNA or fingerprints on the

> rear-view mirror of a car, for instance, doesn't automatically implicate a person in that crime.'"

He also doesn't mention that the panties JonBenet had on were many sizes too large for her. JonBenet wore a size six. The panties found on her were size twelve. They had been bought for an older cousin. Now are we to believe that a pedophile killer would redress his victim at all, much less root though her dressers for a pair of undies much too large?

Smit's interview of John Ramsey was largely uneventful. In his book, Det. Thomas describes it:

> *The June 1998 interview with Patsy and John Ramsey defined them, in my opinion ...*
>
> *Smit appeared to telegraph his questions, giving Ramsey plenty of information before asking for an answer, therefore allowing him plenty of time to consider what he was about to say. Smit even suggested that the cellar room had been recently swept and thus the Hi-Tec print was new. Yes, John Ramsey confirmed —indeed it had been recently swept.*
>
> *... His interview, of course, was predicated on the idea that the Ramseys were innocent, and his bias was obvious.*
>
> *... Smit also seemed to lose control of the interview at times and let John Ramsey question him. Ramsey asked about the stun gun, and Smit went on the videotaped record by saying that yes, he though a stun gun had been used. It was a terrible mistake because a defense attorney would be able to show the jury that a district attorney's own investigator believed an alternate theory of the crime.*

Is it any wonder why Thomas threw the remote at the monitor and screamed, "he's controlling the fucking investigation!" in a rage?

Oddly enough, Smit pointed out that the "intruder" had pulled a chair against the door of the window room, blocking the way. Smit cast doubt on his own theory, to which John Ramsey admitted that the intruder left no good evidence behind. (John has also said this was, quote, "an inside job." No argument here.) It didn't even faze Mr. Super Sleuth.

I think it's helpful to remember that for all of this talk about what a great homicide detective Lou Smit is, his record of over 200 homicides solved is due to several factors. Number one, he never solved them alone. He always worked with a team, not as a lone wolf. Secondly, the great majority of the murders he dealt with were open-and-shut cases. Uneducated killers who barely had enough sense to drop the gun, as it were. He'd never handled anyone like John and Patsy Ramsey. Thirdly, his own wife at the time was suffering from cancer. I regret to say that she has since passed away. When he saw that Patsy had fought it and lived through it, maybe he felt some projected affection. Maybe he figured no one who survived cancer could kill. Fourthly, he admits that he has almost no experience with staging. He said in 2000 that only two of the cases he worked involved staging and that it was very minimal. So he really wouldn't know what to look for.

Smit is as admired by the pro-Ramsey camp as Det. Thomas is hated. As an illustration of how far they will go to tip the historical balance in Smit's favor, Steve Thomas has often taken heat for the fact that he shot a berserk, knife-wielding man during his time as a SWAT officer. But those people never mention how Lou Smit also shot a man in 1972. The man Smit shot was unarmed and attempting to run away. Big hero.

In 1998, Smit quit the DA's office when a Grand Jury was convened. That meant he had to turn over the case file evidence that he was working with. The DA dragged its feet, allowing him time to copy it onto his computer, making a Power Point presentation. Smit's request to testify before the Grand Jury was denied by Michael Kane, who demanded that Smit return the evidence he had illegally copied. Smit went to a lawyer friend of his, cooked up a cockamamie story about the DA's office wanting to destroy evidence (a filthy lie repeated *ad nauseam* by Tracey, Wood and Bennett in their attempt to portray Michael Kane as unethical and overzealous), and won the right to keep it. Hunter, afraid of the implications, allowed him to keep it and to testify. Hunter and Smit reached their agreement on October 1, 1999, saying that he could share it with anyone he chose. Apparently, Smit's lawyers blackmailed Hunter by threatening to reveal that Hunter had been leaking sensitive information to the "Globe" tabloid in an attempt to attack John Eller. Assistant DA Bill Wise said he had no worries about Smit misusing the evidence. Define "misuse," Bill. Exactly what would you consider misuse of information/ evidence in an open murder case? Giving it to the prime suspects? Parsing out selected evidence out to the media to proclaim the prime suspects innocent and smear the BPD? Using it to promote himself as the "expert" in this case while twisting and misstating the facts as often as he can on TV and even under oath to support the prime suspects in a deposition used to get a dismissal of a civil case? Using that originally stolen Power Point to destroy this case forever by putting it in the hands of a numb skull like Michael Tracey? The Governor of Colorado at the time, Bill Owens, said he saw no need to appoint a special prosecutor after the Grand

Jury debacle. Had he known about this little backroom shakedown, he might have changed his mind.

Ironically, Smit's mantra is "the obvious is usually the right answer." I don't regret taking his advice. I just wish he had.

For my part, Lou Smit is a big reason why no one has had to answer for JonBenet's death. He allowed himself to be taken in by a couple of ruthless manipulators and supplied them with evidence that he took illegally. He should not have been allowed to remain on the case when his biases became obvious, and he should have gone to jail. As far as I'm concerned he can go to hell.

Lou Smit passed away on August 11, 2010 from colon cancer at the age of 75. For him, this case will always be the one that got away. How much he had to do with that is, I suppose, a matter of opinion. Whatever his legacy ends up being, good or bad, he earned it.

CHAPTER NINE

Judge Carnes' Carnival of Errors

When their book was published in 2000, the Ramseys were taken to court by several people they named as suspects. Many of these people were represented by Darnay Hoffman, a New York-based lawyer who had been trying to get the Ramseys in court for quite a while. One was former Ramsey housekeeper Linda Hoffmann-Pugh. Her case went nowhere when Hoffman missed several court dates. When Robert Christian Wolf sued them, Hoffman decided to represented him. Wolf might have been better off if Hoffman had no-showed then, as well.

Hoffman is best known as the lawyer who defended the "Subway vigilante" Bernard Goetz, and as the husband of Sydney Biddle Barrows, the "Mayflower Madam." When the Wolf case found its way before Atlanta federal judge Julie Carnes, Hoffman had convinced Wolf that it wasn't just enough for him to say that he hadn't killed JonBenet and prove he was a libeled man, but that Patsy Ramsey knew he couldn't have done it because she did it. This changed the dynamic of the case where Wolf would have to prove she did it. He had one thing going for him. In civil court, the burden of proof is not "beyond a reasonable doubt." It's whoever can present the most evidence.

In March 2003, Judge Carnes made a summary judgment on the case. It would not go before a jury. Carnes' report stated that the evidence was more consistent with an intruder than with Patsy having done it. Naturally, this was and is a huge propaganda coup for the Ramseys and Lin Wood. Trouble is, it collapses very quickly upon close inspection. Judge Carnes could only rule on the evidence presented to her. Since Hoffman didn't have the actual police case file, which he tried like hell to get, he had to rely on his own experts. Sadly, this was not enough against the evidence the Ramseys presented, thanks to Lou Smit. The judge's report lists countless points that the Ramseys asserted that could have been challenged, but weren't, including the stun gun, JonBenet's chronic abuse, the knot evidence, and so on. Since Hoffman made no attempt to challenge many of those points, the judge had to accept them as true. Carnes knew nothing about the fiber evidence, the pathologist reports, or anything else like that. Hoffman had tried to get Cyril Wecht and Robert Stratbucker to testify, but they withdrew, leaving him in the cold.

During the case, Steve Thomas, Chief Beckner, Lou Smit and Alex Hunter were deposed in court. Lin Wood pulled off a real coup when he got Thomas talking about the FBI's involvement. Thomas said that one of the strategies the FBI suggested was to mount a media campaign against the Ramseys in order to force them to confess. While this is a fairly standard ploy in cases like this, it allows the Ramseys and their supporters to claim that none of the reported evidence against them is real. It's too bad Kane wasn't deposed.

The biggest claim accepted by the judge was the claim that Patsy was cleared as the writer of the ransom note. In their book, the Ramseys claim that Patsy was ranked a 4.5

out of 5 by the experts who studied the ransom note, 1 being a match, 5 being complete elimination. Alex Hunter seemed to confirm this in his deposition. The truth is much more damaging for the Ramseys. For starters, no such 1-5 scale exists. In *US v. Thorton*, it was established that a nine-point scale was generally accepted. It reads, from 1 to 9, Identification, Highly probable did write, Probably did write, Indications did write, No conclusion, Indications did not write, Probably did not write, Highly probable did not write, and Elimination A four would put her at "indications did write." According to Det. Thomas, the 1-5 scale was developed by two experts hired by the Ramseys, Howard Rile and Lloyd Cunningham. Three days after Thomas's comments, Hunter referred to the scale as "mumbo-jumbo." It strikes me as odd that not even her own paid experts could rule her out.

The four experts hired by the Boulder Police Department and DA's office all had different opinions, placing Patsy anywhere from "she wrote it" to "I can't tell." Only one came anywhere near elimination. Richard Dusak, from the Secret Service, said he saw no evidence that she wrote it. But in *Perfect Murder, Perfect Town*, Schiller writes that he made his decision early on before the experts had a full range of Patsy Ramsey's exemplars to work with. And it has been wondered just how much document analysis he actually performs, since it's not his primary duty. As Chet Ubowski, the examiner from the Colorado Bureau of Investigation and the man who did the most extensive analysis said, they would need "the full range of her handwriting." In *Perfect Murder, Perfect Town*, Ubowski told his boss, Peter Mang, that he believed Patsy Ramsey wrote it, but he couldn't say so with courtroom certainty. In 2002, Ubowski was reported by FOX News to say that only the bleeding ink from the felt-tip pen and the disguised letters kept him from saying she wrote it. As Steve Thomas said, "out of 74 people whose writing was examined, Patsy was the only person who set off alarm bells."

Worse, none of them knew at the time that Patsy was ambidextrous. In 2000, Patsy was asked if she could write left-handed. She said she could, but not very well. Later that year, Linda Hoffmann-Pugh and one of Patsy's art teachers said she was fairly proficient at left-handed writing. Another thing they had against them was the note was written with a broad felt-tip Sharpie, which is less than ideal for analysis. Since it had been used over time, that would distort it even more. The more a pen like that is used, the more worn down the tip gets. It starts to lose it's rounded point and becomes flatter. Since the pen was most likely locked up in some evidence room, Patsy would have had to write her exemplars with a different one. That would make a change right away. Lastly, the letter was block-printed, which is extremely difficult to analyze. It's a classic method of disguising one's handwriting.

Edwin Alford said he couldn't be sure, but he said that he couldn't rule her out. Leonard Speckin said he couldn't say she wrote it either, but conceded that it was unlikely that anyone could have had as many similarities. But Carnes saw preliminary reports that Smit had and used them to claim that Patsy didn't write the note. It's possible that none of them wanted to go up against Howard Rile in court. Handwriting analysis is a very small community. Nobody wants to make too many waves, especially against Rile, who is highly respected. Add to that, a lot of professional document examiners tend to be cautious anyway.

To offset this, Hoffman and Wolf hired their own experts. Tom Miller, who I mentioned earlier was one. David Leibman, president of the National Association of Document Examiners, said he found fifty-one similarities and was 90-95% certain she wrote it. Cina Wong, who had worked for John Grisham and Bank of America and has roughly the same experience as Ubowski said she was certain she wrote it. Donald Lacy, Richard Williams and Larry Ziegler also said she wrote it.

It should be noted that none of these experts had access to the original note and had to work from copies. That limited their value somewhat. Also, only three of Hoffman's experts were certified by the American Board of Forensic Document Examiners, one of the recognized organizations for accrediting handwriting experts. That doesn't stop courts from using non-ABFDE members' testimony, but it helps. Chet Ubowski, Richard Dusak, Leonard Speckin, Edwin Alford, and Howard Rile are members. Hoffman's ABFDE examiners were Larry Ziegler, Richard Williams and Gideon Epstein.

I think it's helpful to remember that the ABFDE's position at top of the heap is largely due to the way they politicked their way to that spot, not so much because they are the end-all, be-all they claim to be. They have a vested interest in keeping non-ABFDE members out of the loop. If a non-ABFDE member is accepted in court, that would undercut the ABFDE's status, and the big money contracts that come with it. All that should matter is who the courts recognize and allow to testify as an expert. It doesn't matter what propaganda a given organization choses to spread, the fact of the matter is that if a court accepts your qualifications, you're qualified. That includes NADE, ABFDE and others.

The Ramseys and their supporters have made the claim that only the ABFDE is acceptable by court standards, but it's patently false. The ABFDE website lists no such claim.

The following sums up the reality of the situation:

> *Certification is not required in order for a document examiner to qualify in court as an expert, but is does assist in identifying experts who have been tested and found to be knowledgeable in the field. Most certifying organizations require written and/ or oral testing. The organizations that certify their members Include NADE, WADE, NQDA, IAQDE, AFDE, and ABFDE.*
>
> Attorney's Guide to Document Examination
> By Katherine Koppenhaver, page 6

Regardless, Hoffman was again dealt a bad hand. Miller, Williams, Lacy, and Liebman were not called to testify. Larry Ziegler got into a conflict of personalities with Hoffman and refused to testify, even though he believed Patsy to have written it. Hoffman, nevertheless, continued with two outstanding experts, Epstein and Wong.

Gideon Epstein said at the trial that because Wong was not a member of ABFDE, her testimony was worthless. He has since reconsidered that view. But Epstein himself is another story. Epstein is a forensic document examiner who served as the past president of the American Society of Questioned Document Examiners, is a registered member of the ABFDE, and has authored several authoritative texts in the field. Epstein has appeared in 200 cases over a thirty year period, having examined thousands of documents and has established questioned document laboratories for not only the US government, but for those of Eastern Europe and the Philippines as well, while teaching hundreds of government document examiners their professions. When Hoffman hired him, he had just retired from twenty years as the head of document examination for the Immigration and Naturalization Service, where he had been responsible for tracking down war criminals who had slipped into the United States using false names in the years following World War Two. His most notable catch was Valerian Trifa, an officer in the Iron Guard, Romanian fascists who took over their country and allied with Hitler. The Iron Guard were active participants in the Holocaust. Most people agree that Epstein is one of the world's best, and Judge Carnes ruled that he was qualified to give an opinion. His opinion was that he was, quote, "absolutely certain" (which he clarified in follow-up questioning to mean "100 percent certain") Patsy Ramsey wrote the ransom letter. Judge Carnes' ruling does something of a tap-dance on the question of Epstein, noting that only a jury and not a judge can find him credible or not. But she said that in his deposition in the case Epstein hadn't explained the methodology he had used to conclude with "absolute certainty" that Patsy had written the note. Yes, he had said there were similarities between the note and Patsy Ramsey's handwriting, but he hadn't specified how many similarities or what kind of similarities they were. His failure to do so, Judge Carnes concluded, meant that "the weight and impact" of his testimony would "necessarily" have been less than the weight of the handwriting experts relied on by Boulder police. Of course, there were no attempts made by Hoffman to ask him how he arrived at his conclusions. Epstein also said that in thirty years of testifying in court cases, this was the first time he had not been allowed to use comparison charts, which would have gone a long way towards establishing him. He also said that his attempts to obtain original exemplars from the Ramseys were refused.

It should also be noted that the majority of opinion stands today that whoever wrote the captions in the Ramsey family photo album wrote the ransom letter. Patsy Ramsey, when deposed, claimed not to recognize her own handwriting. When she did so, Patsy used the phrase "not particularly", again straight out of the ransom note, as well as "particularly". The ransom letter phrase is "The two gentlemen looking over your daughter do (and the word "not" was inserted here with an inverted v) not particularly like your daughter." Here are her exact words:

Q: *I would like you to now look at the handwriting below the photograph. Do you recognize the handwriting?*

A: *Not particularly.*

Q. *You say "not particularly." You don't recognize this as being your handwriting; is that correct?*

A. *I don't remember writing it. Is that what you mean? I mean, I don't know. I may have, but–*

Q: *I will go to the next question. Do you recognize any of the handwriting as being your handwriting?*

A. *Not particularly.*

Q. *So you couldn't say, with any degree of certainty, that–that was your handwriting?*

A. *No.*

Q. *Thank you.*

From a different section of the deposition:

Q. *Were you concerned about that?*

A. *I was not concerned, particularly.*

From another section of the deposition:

Q. *Is there anything about the Bs that to you looks similar beside the fact they are lower case? The way they are drawn?*

A. *No, not particularly.*

The video footage of Patsy's deposition was later studied by Colorado radio personality Jann Scott. According to him, upon being asked "do you recognize this handwriting," Patsy shook her head yes, possibly in a subconscious acknowledgment of guilt.

Also, the Ramseys have never released the reports done by their own experts, or anyone else for that matter. They release everything else. What are they hiding? In 2006, during the media frenzy over John Mark Karr, Darnay Hoffman pointed out that the Ramseys had never released their handwriting reports publically, whereas they had released anything else that helped their case. In John Ramsey's deposition, Hoffman confronted Lin Wood with that knowledge. Wood said that he would do exactly that: make the reports public and shut Hoffman up. That never happened. A clue as to why that did not happen may be found in the deposition. Wood claims that he asked Hal Haddon, the Ramsey criminal lawyer for the reports, but Haddon wouldn't give them to him. Haddon cited Grand Jury secrecy laws. In mid-2001, Hoffman got a judge to rule Colorado's Grand Jury secrecy laws unconstitutional. Wood tried again after that ruling, and Haddon still wouldn't give them up. So I ask again: what are they hiding? It doesn't help that both of Patsy's sisters and her own mother couldn't tell the difference between her handwriting and the writing on the ransom letter. Even worse is that she was the only person who changed her writing after the crime.

Cherokee, a frequent poster at www.forumsforjustice.org, has compiled an extensive analysis, which can be accessed at: http://www.forumsforjustice.org/forums/showthread.php?t=6404

A sample of the charts that Epstein was not allowed to use can be accessed through www.forumsforjustice.com

In short, Judge Carnes had no choice but to rule the way she did. The Ramseys didn't hurt Hoffman and Wolf so much as they hurt themselves with their hubris. Everyone knew, or should have known, what was at stake here: if Hoffman and Wolf had gotten past summary judgment and gotten before a jury, they would have essentially been able to put the Ramseys on trial for the murder of JonBenet, with the libel case as a fig leaf. And they would have been able to do it without having to meet the standard of "beyond a reasonable doubt." Instead, the Ramseys get a propaganda windfall, Wolf gets nothing, and Mary Lacy gets someone on her side. But Carnes overstepped her bounds. She had no call to claim the evidence showed the Ramseys to be innocent when she hadn't seen all of it.

To sum up, it was truly a courtroom comedy of errors. It should have been so sweet, too; so easy to prove Patsy did it. But it turned out to be the last time anyone would get the Ramseys in court again. In 2004, a lawsuit that the Ramseys had filed against FOX News for a story in 2002 went before a judge in Colorado. The rules were different there. In a

Colorado court, settlements have a cap, so a plaintiff can only demand so much. Instead of letting it go before a jury, the judge ruled that the Ramseys had no grounds to sue FOX News. The FOX lawyers didn't make the same mistakes that Hoffman did. They petitioned the DA's office to get the entire case file, and several Boulder newspapers supported them. Turns out they didn't need the file after all. I'm kind of sorry the case didn't go forward, but that's life.

CHAPTER TEN

Lies, Liars and the Lying Lie Detectors Who Test Them

In May of 2000, the Ramseys announced to the press that they had passed a polygraph, known as a lie detector test. It was quickly revealed that the tests were in and of themselves a big lie.

A little history of polygraphs is in order. Invented in the 1940s by William Moulton Marston, the creator of comic book heroine Wonder Woman, polygraphs measure the body's natural responses to telling a lie: heart rate, breathing, the lot. But over time, they have come under fire. Polygraphs work on the premise that everyone has a conscience, that little voice that tells you when you're doing something wrong. When you lie, the theory goes, your conscience causes involuntary bodily reactions, which the polygraph measures. It doesn't read a person's mind. Because of this, there are certain problems with it. The biggest problem is a false positive. That's when a polygraph says you're lying when you're really telling the truth. It happens more frequently than you might expect. People get overly anxious, scared, whatever. I personally don't believe in polygraphs. Even if I knew I was innocent I wouldn't take one. There's plenty of literature that will support me. There's a reason why polygraphs aren't admissible in court: they're not sufficiently reliable.

But there's another problem. It is possible to beat the machine. See, polygraph tests depend as much on the person conducting the tests as they do on the machine itself. A good polygrapher will know what to do if he thinks there's a false positive. He will try to correct it.. It's more difficult to see a false negative. For someone to beat the machine, there are several ways to do it. The most well-known is the person who is a pathological liar, someone to whom lying is no big deal. The most famous person to beat it is Ted Bundy, the serial killer. He passed a polygraph easily, because he had no conscience. Less well known are the other ways. One way is self-deception. Josef Goebbles, the Nazi propaganda minister, once said that if a lie is told often enough, it will be accepted as truth. What he didn't mention is that if a person lies to himself or herself long enough, they might start to believe it. Anthony Pietropinto is a psychiatrist who wrote that if someone uses circular reasoning, they can convince themselves of anything and beat a polygraph. If you take a polygraph, and you say something that is false, as long as you believe it to be true, you won't be lying. More inventive is substitution. If someone asks you a question, you just substitute the question in your mind with one you know is true. For example, if someone were to ask me, "is your name David," which they would do to establish a baseline, and I substituted that with "do I own a luxury yacht" and answered "no," it would come out as truthful. Right now I can picture a whole slew of cops and federal agents reading this screaming, "Jesus Christ! Don't say that!" But I think it's better to expose all of this stuff so that polygraphs will finally be relegated to the junk pile they belong in.

Here's where the Ramseys come in. From 1997 on, they were asked if they would take a polygraph. Sometimes one would agree, other times not. But it never took place. In 2000, Chief Mark Beckner made them an offer: take a polygraph. If you pass, we'll clear you as suspects. If you fail, we can't use it anyway. The Ramseys said no, claiming the police were out to trap them. Beckner offered to have the test conducted by a veteran of the FBI. That was also unacceptable to them. They claimed that the FBI was part of the conspiracy against them (sure they were!). The police wouldn't budge. So, the Ramseys bought their own test.

The first person they contacted was Gene Parker. He was interested, but said that he would have to insist on a drug test because the issue was so serious. He said he would pay, out of his own pocket, for a team of doctors and nurses to perform urine tests right on the premises. Lin Wood said he'd get back to Parker. Three hours later, he did. He told Parker they wouldn't need him. They found someone else who didn't require drug tests. Trouble is, Wood had already said on *Larry King Live* that they would submit to drug tests:

> PHONE CALLER: *I just want to say I think it's wonderful that they've agreed to take a polygraph test. And my question is, would they also submit to a blood test to make sure they were not taking anything, i.e., medication, herbs, that would alter their response to the questions on the polygraph? How would you answer that, sir?*

> LIN WOOD: *Oh, absolutely. I'm sure that the question would be asked if they're on any medications, and they would answer that question truthfully and submit to any urinalysis that was required or asked of them.*

I guess talk is cheap.

Jerry Toriello is a polygrapher based in New Jersey. The Ramseys settled on him. The Ramseys were put through a battery of tests by Toriello and neither John nor Patsy was able to pass. The best Toriello could do for the Ramseys was label the tests, "inconclusive" and suggest they seek out the services of a different polygrapher The sting in that tale is that an expert polygrapher isn't supposed to give up that easily. If a test does come back inconclusive, the polygrapher will redouble his efforts, modifying the test questions to eliminate doubt. So you have to ask what made Toriello tell them to go elsewhere. Could it be that he was afraid "inconclusive" was the best he'd get? And that they'd only come out more deceptive if he tried again? Based on everything we know, I'd say that's likely. But it will have to remain conjecture because whatever Toriello saw, he can't talk about it. When an attorney contracts for a polygraph test, he will have the examiner sign a confidentiality agreement. And Toriello has never spoken about it. We may never know for sure, but according to Ed Gelb, the polygrapher the Ramseys finally settled on, when you buy a polygraph test you specify the results you want. And if getting those results isn't possible, make sure the truth is protected from reaching the public. No attorney worth his retainer will have his client(s) take a polygraph without knowing how they're going to do; he doesn't want to be accused of malpractice.

After the results of the polygraph they finally did take, Wood claimed that it was a lie that they had turned down an examiner who had insisted on a drug test.. We know that's false.

Once Ed Gelb entered the picture, things got even weirder. Ed Gelb has served as president, executive director and chairman of the board of the American Polygraph Association and is an honorary fellow of the Academy of Certified Polygraphists. Gelb was trained in polygraph technique at the Backster School of Lie Detection, founded by Cleve Backster of San Diego. Gelb claims to have performed over 30,000 polygraph examinations. While Gelb may or may not be considered the foremost polygraph examiner in the country, he certainly is the most well-known, having appeared over the years on several TV programs. Once he got involved in this case, his background fell under scrutiny. Gelb claims to have received his doctorate from LaSalle University in Louisiana. That's bad, because LaSalle was found to be a fraud. Thomas Kirk, the man who founded LaSalle, was arrested by the FBI and was found guilty of fraud and sentenced to five years in federal prison. Kirk earned millions of dollars from people looking to obtain fraudulent college degrees at a discount rate with little or no actual course work needed. Sounds like the man who detects deception is a master of it himself. His main claim to fame is that he found several people who claimed to have been abducted by aliens to be truthful. One such incident served as the inspiration for the movie *Fire In the Sky*.

I mentioned that a man named Cleve Backster was Gelb's mentor. Backster actually participated in the Ramsey tests in what was called "quality control." You see, Backster developed the system used for the numerical evaluation of polygraph tests which he called the "Backster Zone Comparison" polygraph technique. Ed Gelb ran the actual polygraph machine and asked the questions, and his buddy Backster scored the finished tests based on the numerical standards he had developed. However, Backster's background is also troubled. In the late 1970s, he claimed his polygraph machine could read the emotions of plants and that the plants could read his mind. He later extended the experiment to living human cells. This new work of Backster's has been published in a book titled, "Secret Life of Your Cells: The Latest From Cleve Backster`s Research", by Robert B. Stone.

Patsy Ramsey once referred to lie detectors as "voodoo science." I guess she must have always believed that because she and her husband hired two of the best damn witch-doctors in the business. When commenting on the Ramsey tests, F. Lee Bailey (Gelb's old buddy from the television program days and one of OJ Simpson's lawyers during his murder trial) claims that, "after 45 years he doesn't know how to beat a lie detector test, or any examiner who knows how to beat it." Oh, yeah? Maybe Bailey should sit down with former police polygrapher Doug Gene Williams, who knows how to beat the lie detector and sells an illustrated manual entitled, "How to Sting the Polygraph".

From a technical standpoint, the Ramsey polygraph had more problems. In her book, *And Justice For Some,* Wendy Murphy points out that "a proper question should be short and shouldn't contain words that have loose meanings. For example, a good question would be 'did you kill JonBenet?' Not much wiggle room. Instead, the Ramseys were asked long, murky questions like 'Regarding JonBenet, do you know for sure who killed her?' Adding extra words and fuzzy terms like 'regarding' and 'for sure' gives the test subject's mind time and space to wander. Short direct questions force the subject to focus."

She also mentions a part of the polygraph that often is overlooked by those not in the know: the pre-test interview. It's not known today what the pre-test interview for the

Ramseys was like, or if there even was one. During a pre-test interview, the examiner will, ideally, get the subject to focus. It's also a good opportunity for the examiner to show that he is aware of the facts of the case, which tells the subject, "don't try anything or I'll know." Lastly, it gets the subject's memory working. One gets the feeling this is what the Ramseys were afraid of when the FBI test was offered.

And at the end of the day, it took Patsy three attempts to get a reading close enough where Gelb could say she passed. Anybody can pass a test if they take it enough times. Like Chris Rock says, "Passed it. Got a 65!" Any halfway intelligent suspect can beat it when they have three years-plus practice time. Oddly enough, the only member of the news media to smell a rat in the first few days was Katie Couric. Couric is usually such an ass-clown for the Ramseys, it's embarrassing to watch her interviews with them and especially their lawyer Lin Wood. If anyone sucked my ass that hard, my head would collapse. So it was somewhat shocking when she asked them how legitimate the lie detector tests could be since they were paid for by the Ramseys. Patsy Ramsey got a little pissy about that. That seems to happen a lot when she doesn't get things her way. Makes you wonder even more about that night, doesn't it?

In short, too little, too late.

CHAPTER ELEVEN

From Myth to Reality

When a case like this happens, it doesn't take long for rumors to spring up and spread. In this case, where you have the police, the DA and the prime suspects all waging media wars against the others in a three-way dance of death, that just makes it worse. Add to that all the time that has passed and sometimes myth overwhelms reality. Right now, I'd like to clear up some of the more prevalent ones.

One of the earliest and most widespread stories was that the police found no footprints in the snow when they canvassed the house that morning. While technically true, there were large areas on the lawn that had no snow on them. The concrete walkways were also clear. The deal breaker here is that there was frost everywhere. Now, faithful reader, I ask you to do this: the next really cold night in your area, take a very quick walk out on a frosty patch of grass. The idea is that the frozen grass will leave detectable footprints. Then go out in the morning before it gets too late. See if you can still see them.

Melody Stanton, a nearby neighbor, initially told police that she heard a scream shortly after midnight and that it sounded like a little girl. A series of tests were conducted. It was found that a scream from the basement could be heard better outside than inside on the third floor. But how would an intruder know that? He'd get the hell out of Dodge. Later, Stanton said she couldn't be sure if she's actually heard JonBenet's death scream or the "negative spiritual energy" of her death.

One myth put out by the Ramseys for very obviously self-serving reasons is the notion, repeated by their lawyers and PIs as fact, is that the police focused solely on the parents as suspects and ignored evidence of an intruder. Alex Hunter himself seems to have implied this on a few occasions. In truth, many of the so-called "leads" that were never followed up on were generated by Team Ramsey itself as part of their "keep the parents out of jail" initiative. The police formally interviewed over 600 people, investigated over 150 suspects, including one who was serving time in North Carolina, and built up a case file of over 60,000 pages. Sounds like they were pretty serious about following leads. Henry Lee, in 2002, said he could guarantee that every scenario was explored. Lee was deep in the DA's office. After his "clearing" by the DA in July 2008, John Ramsey repeated this lie and has been allowed to get away with it. He and his wife created this lie to make themselves look like martyrs. Ramsey supporters have often said that they were suspects because they didn't act like Middle Americans expect grieving parents to act. John says he doesn't know how a grieving parent is supposed to act. Well, allow me to clue you in. Brenda and Damon Van Dam and Ed Smart and Marc Klaas were suspected early on in the disappearances of their children, as well. But the cops and most American that I know never seriously suspected them. They turned out to be innocent. Do you know why no one suspected them after a while? Because they didn't whine about how badly they were being treated by the police and the media like John and Patsy did. They always talked about how important their daughters were, and didn't refer to them as "that child," like the Ramseys did, as if they couldn't be bothered to remember her name. All the Ramseys ever did was whine and complain. Another lie John told was that he and Patsy accepted the fact that they would be investigated, and that it was only when the police stopped looking at other people that he got upset. We know that's a lie because John Ramsey himself said that he and Patsy were, and I quote, "insulted" that they would be suspected, because we all know it's only those skanky, blue-collar people who do that kind of stuff. He expects us to believe this nonsense. What arrogance! I realize I'm not being objective here, but it's an insult to my intelligence and yours as readers to hear this stuff when it's patently untrue. And he has a lot of nerve whining about being a suspect when he and his wife were so willing to point the finger at other people. Especially when those "skanky, blue-collar people" would make up the jury that would have tried them.

A letter was supposedly received by police from Shreveport, Louisiana. According to the story, it was from a little girl who had been in a pageant with JonBenet. Her mother had helped her write it. The story holds that JonBenet confided in this girl that someone had hurt her private place. Nothing ever came of this story.

Patsy Ramsey claimed that JonBenet's pageants were not a big part of her life and that she wanted to do them. In 2006, John Ramsey claimed that he always hated the pageants and Patsy was very insistent upon them, even when JonBenet was less than enthusiastic. Which is true?

Early on, it was theorized by some in the media that John Ramsey had child pornography ties. The only evidence was his frequent trips to Amsterdam, which is known as a pornography capital. The house was searched, but it has never been revealed what was found or what wasn't. To speculate, if there were anything, we probably would have heard by now.

It was alleged that pictures of JonBenet and Burke in the nude were found in the Michigan home. No confirmation has ever come out. Even if said pictures were to exist, having naked pictures of one's own children is not that unusual.

One that Team Ramsey keeps repeating is that the DNA found was from a white person. DNA science is not yet advanced enough to tell race, if race can be determined from DNA at all, according to the Human Genome Project.

In their book *Death of Innocence*, the Ramseys claim that pictures of JonBenet were retouched by unscrupulous media outlets in order to make her look even more garishly made up than she was, supposedly to make the Ramseys look trashier, thus more guilty. But Judith Phillips, who took many of the photographs, including the one with Patsy, JonBenet, Burke and Nedra, claims that they were completely legit and Patsy insisted on it.

These are just a few stories not based in fact. Some were created legitimately through misinterpretation or misunderstanding. Others were deliberate attempts to muddy the water.

CHAPTER TWELVE

Pick Your Perp

In the world of the Internet subculture that has sprung up around this case, which I've been touching on throughout this book, it seems like every person you talk to has a different theory of the case and crime. I'd like to use this space to share a few of them with you now.

To this day, some interesting theories as to who really killed JonBenet Ramsey. Many include evidence from one side, others from the other, and some are just out there.

In his book, Detective Thomas wrote that he thought Patsy Ramsey did everything alone and killed JonBenet over her constant bedwetting. What set him on that path was this: to hear him tell it, there was a red turtleneck that JonBenet wore sometimes balled up in the sink in JonBenet's bedroom. Supposedly, Patsy had wanted JonBenet to wear it to the Whites' party Christmas night so they would match. Whether or not she actually wore it is up for debate, since, to my knowledge, no pictures have ever surfaced of JonBenet from that party. Thomas believed that JonBenet wore that turtleneck to bed and Patsy stripped it off when JonBenet wet her bed that night. In his account, Patsy was shown a photo of that balled-up shirt and couldn't help crying.

Dale Yeager of SERAPH said that Patsy Ramsey was a religious zealot who had used sexual abuse to keep JonBenet in line and finally killed her for being "sinful."

Along those lines psychiatrist Carole Lieberman and psychotherapist Jamie Turndorf allege Patsy might have killed JonBenet for the same reason that the Wicked Queen fed a poison apple to Snow White: so she could be fairest in the land again.

Darnay Hoffman theorized she killed JonBenet because of depression.

Diane Hollis, an employee at Access Graphics along with John Ramsey, thought that Patsy had caught John in the act of molesting JonBenet, swung at him and hit her by accident.

Dr. Rusty Morris took what Michael Kane said to the next step, alleging that Patsy suffered from Munchausen-by-Proxy Syndrome which caused her to use her daughter to get attention and finally killed her to get worldwide sympathy.

Others allege a religious sacrifice.

A select few think Patsy was suffering from multiple personality disorder and possessed by a hostile personality that hated JonBenet.

John is a favorite target, with some, like Cyril Wecht believing that he killed JonBenet in a sex game that went too far.

Or he killed her to keep her silent about abuse.

Or that he and his friends (which, depending on the theory you hear, include Mike Bynum, Fleet White, Dr. Beuf, John Fernie and others) were running a child pornography ring.

Burke Ramsey is a surprising favorite. Even though he was only nine years old, it's speculated that he killed JonBenet by accident because he didn't know any better. It's been guessed that he suffered from autism or Asperger's Syndrome, but nothing has ever come of that. Another idea is that he hit JonBenet because he was mad at her, his anger caused by jealousy. Yet another alleges that Burke had heard of a choking game at school (the kind we see being talked about on the *Dr. Phil* show, for example), tried it out on JonBenet and accidentally choked her to death. More outrageous theories have Burke and a friend, possibly Doug Stine, who was considerably older, fooling around and spiraling out of control. In just about all of these, John or Patsy or both are alleged to have helped cover for him. This scenario holds appeal for some because it allows people to believe in the family's basic innocence: they've lost one child. Now they will protect the other one.

John Andrew Ramsey was never a serious suspect from the police standpoint, but some people wondered if he was JonBenet's abuser, since a blanket with his semen on it was found inside a suitcase in the basement. Either that, or he resented Patsy, who he described as "flashy," for taking away his father and sought to hurt her by killing her precious daughter and framing her for the crime.

The jealousy theme sometimes extends to other members of the family, including Melinda Ramsey and Pamela Paugh (my mother's favorite suspect).

Once you get into the realm of intruder suspects, things get even more fascinating. Generally speaking, you have three distinct categories of intruder suspects. The first is pedophiles. Generally, they are divided on whether or not JonBenet's participation in pageants had anything to do with it. Some think they did. One on-line writer who does not subscribe to the intruder theory (to say the least) calls these pageants "pedophilic livestock shows." To me, it's like putting out bacon for wolves. Others think that pageants don't figure into it because, the reasoning goes, pedophiles prefer children who look like children, not children who are dressed up like adults. Whatever. Like I said, sometimes you try to get into the heads of creeps and you come out thinking no amount of soap in the world will get you clean again. The second category involves a ransom kidnapping that went terribly wrong. The third involves a revenge killing over a slight, real or imagined, committed either by John or Patsy.

Odd thing is, a lot of these people were named as suspects by the Ramseys and their legal attack dogs, despite their stating that they didn't know anyone "that evil." I guess that platitude went out the window, because they started naming all kinds of people... but only the people who didn't go along with their intruder fantasy. Hmm, I wonder why that is?

"Santa" Bill McReynolds was the chief suspect in the DA's office, according to Schiller and Thomas. He and his wife were suspected because of Janet's play, and because of something JonBenet supposedly said. It is claimed that JonBenet was bragging about an extra visit from Santa after Christmas. Even McReynold's son Jesse was suspected, due to his criminal record (minor stuff). Bill McReynolds died in 2002.

Fleet White Jr. is a perennial suspect.

He was a neighbor, he had changed JonBenet's underwear at his house and he was known to play nasty tricks on his daughter Daphne, such as hiding from her. That actually played into the search that morning. One day, Daphne had hidden from her father. He searched his house for her and was near panic when she came out and said, "here I am, Daddy!" His efforts to bring in special investigators to crack down on the Ramseys is seen by some as an effort to throw up a smoke screen. His wife Priscilla is named in a few theories as an accomplice.

Linda Hoffmann-Pugh, the Ramsey housekeeper and her husband Mervin Pugh, their handyman are suspected by some. They needed the money and they had keys.

Brian Scott was the family gardener. He made a comment about how shapely JonBenet's legs were, so the line of thinking goes he took his interest too far.

Rod Westmoreland was John Ramsey's financial advisor. He might know about the bonus. But he wasn't in the city that night.

Lou Smit supposedly wondered if Doug Stine, son of Ramsey friend Susan Stine, could be involved.

Nedra Paugh, Patsy Ramsey's mother, said that the killer was one of John Ramsey's coworkers. Tom Carson and Jeff Merrick were two.

Once you move beyond the people who were well known to the family, the theories get increasingly bizarre.

Chris Wolf was named by his former girlfriend, Jackie Dilson, who said he was "agitated" about the killing. He also had a hat that said "South Boulder Tennis Club."

Gary Oliva is a pervert who hangs out in Boulder. One of 38 registered sex offenders who live in the area, he is supposed to have spoken to JonBenet earlier that day when she was riding her new bike.

John Gigax was named by Michael Tracey. 'Nuff said.

Michael Helgoth committed suicide after the killing. Some suspect him, and some more think he was murdered by his accomplice to keep him silent and throw off the trail. Tracey thought that John Kenady might have been the accomplice.

Randall Simons was a photographer who took some of JonBenet's most well-known pictures. He was caught wandering naked down a town street.

A popular idea is that a sexual predator spotted JonBenet at a pageant and had to "have her," or a mother whose child lost to JonBenet was upset enough to kill her over it.

Conservative bloggers have suggested that Ward Churchill and the American Indian Movement are responsible.

Others say that the part about a "foreign faction" in the ransom letter is legit and that JonBenet was killed by terrorist kidnappers. Or, more incredibly, remnants of the Thuggee cult of India are suggested as the killers, since there was almost no blood shed and the Thuggee were known to strangle people as human sacrifice to Kali, the bloodthirsty Hindu goddess. Strangling wastes no blood, so Kali would be pleased, delaying the apocalypse for another millennium. If you ask me, these folks have watched *Indiana Jones and the Temple of Doom* too many times.

The only intruder suspect to be arrested for the crime—the only person to be arrested for the crime at all—was Atlanta native John Mark Karr. In August of 2006, he was arrested in Bangkok, Thailand by Thai police working in concert with the Boulder DA's office and the Department of Homeland Security. For several years, he had claimed to anyone who would listen that he was the killer. He said he went to play with her sexually and he killed her by accident. One of the listeners was Michael Tracey. He took the transcribed conversations to the DA and they went after him. Nauseating as it is, it's also helpful to illustrate the kinds of things he told Tracey. He said that he hid under a bed in a room across from JonBenet's bedroom, slipped into her room, woke her up gently, lured her to the basement with his "Gothic box," and while she was engrossed with that, he slipped the cord around her neck, saying it was a necklace. He then claims he tied her arms and used the excess cord length to hang her vertically. Suspended, her arms were incapacitated and out of the way, allowing him to tighten the cord as a strangulation device (presumably like a noose on a gibbet) while he pulled down her long johns and underwear and performed oral sex on her. In his account, he became so engrossed in his activity, he didn't notice that she was suffocating until it was too late. Realizing he'd killed her, instead of vacating the premises, he then claims, horrifyingly, that he stabbed JonBenet's vagina in order to get it to bleed. His motivation for this was so he could drink some of her blood, an act supposedly in line with his pedophilic tendencies combined with a Roman Catholic upbringing. Supposedly he had to pierce her three times. He then claims that he smashed her head just to make sure she was really dead and wouldn't have to live as a brain-dead husk on an artificial respirator for the rest of her life. His story quickly unraveled in the face of forensic evidence. For one thing, JonBenet's wrists had no marks from being hanged or from any kind of struggle against her bonds, as I mentioned. For another thing, the majority of pathologists say that the head blow came first by a large margin. Third, Tracey assumed that the object Karr used to pierce JonBenet's private place was the paintbrush, but the transcripts clearly state that he used something sharp, like a knife or an icepick, though he didn't say what it was. When Tracey told him it would have to be the brush, he changed his story again to say it was. These are only a small sample of the impossibilities of his account. By the time he arrived in Boulder, the gig was pretty much up. They gave him a "thanks for coming. Don't let the door smack you in the ass on the way out." Karr turned out to be a pathetic pervert looking for fame. Tracey was feeding him information to make his confessions halfway accurate. To this day, Karr claims he is the killer. His background serves to give insight as to how he could be the way he is. His mother was psychotic and tried to kill him, a fact he can't admit today. Psychiatrist Dr. Keith Ablow thinks that Karr believes that Patsy Ramsey killed her daughter and his screwed-up relationship with his own mother led him to confess in order to rehabilitate her in the eyes of the public, and rehabilitate his own mother by extension. That's psychiatry for you, though even a blind squirrel will eventually find a nut, no pun intended. From what I can gather, the DA was perfectly happy to go after him for it, regardless of a DNA match or not. The trouble was his story would have had to match up exactly, and it didn't. I guess it speaks to the true incompetence of the DA's office: this guy said he did it, and they weren't even smart enough to frame the guy, which I have no doubt they would have tried if they thought they could have gotten away with it.

In my opinion, Karr is dangerous. Not for what he says he did and clearly did not do, but for what he might do. And we can all thank Mary Lacy for bringing him "home."

The Web site www.jonbenetramsey.pbwiki.com contains a much more comprehensive listing.

CHAPTER THIRTEEN

The JonBenet Syndrome

Since JonBenet's unfortunate death, there have been cases that resemble her case. While nowhere near identical, they do bear enough resemblance to hers to bring her to mind.

One is the disappearance of Sabrina Aisenberg. She was a five-month-old baby who went missing from her home in Florida. Her parents, Marlene and Steve, told police what they knew at first, but then decided they wouldn't talk anymore. They hid behind their Lin Wood-type lawyer, Barry Cohen. It didn't take long for suspicion to fall on them. Talking heads all over the media started likening Sabrina's disappearance and her parents' silence to the Ramsey case. Unfortunately, one of them was Det. Steve Thomas. He mentions in his book how the "bugging" operation he wanted to do to the Ramseys had just broken the Aisenberg case. He refers to how the cops in that case did in fact plant electronic listening devices in the Aisenberg home and, supposedly, picked up a conversation between the Aisenbergs talking about how Steve had killed his daughter while high on cocaine and that Marlene couldn't bear the thought of going to prison. Sadly, when the tapes were played before a judge, he said he couldn't hear anything but static. He dismissed the case, saying the police and prosecutors had shown bad faith. This would come back to haunt Thomas at his deposition. To this day, Sabrina has never been found.

The Aisenbergs used the same tactic the Ramseys did: attack the police. Steve Thomas should have kept his mouth shut about a case he was not part of. And as for the tapes that the judge said show nothing, when they were played on a CBS broadcast, I heard what the cops say they heard clear as a bell. But the Aisenbergs have never been convicted. It's in the wind.

Another one is the disappearance of Madeline McCann. She was a lovely three-year-old British girl who went missing from her parents' hotel room in Portugal in May of 2007. Her parents, Gerry and Kate were vacationing there with Madeline and her younger siblings. One night, Madeline was gone. Her parents had left the children alone while they were out dining. To this day, she's never been found. Like the Ramseys, they claim that the Portuguese cops bungled the case and are now trying to blame them in order to save face, which was later made worse when the case degenerated into an international pissing contest between the Portuguese police, who felt they had reason to suspect the McCanns, and the British authorities who felt some obligation to get behind their hometown kids. The police in Portugal claim that cadaver dogs smelled the scent of a dead person and that Madeline's DNA was found in the trunk of a car the McCanns rented after she disappeared. Again, no one has ever been charged. I really don't know what to think about the McCann case. I don't know much about it. What I do know is that if it were, somehow, to turn out that the Portuguese police are correct, and Kate McCann did accidentally give her daughter a fatal overdose and later covered it up so adamantly (including a visit to Pope Benedict XVI), then the idea that the Ramseys couldn't have done the same thing goes right out the window. That's just a detached observation.

The one that's most disturbing is the case of ten-month-old Jason Midyette. The reason it's so disturbing is because it took place in Boulder, too. In early 2006, little Jason was brought to the Boulder county hospital. He didn't leave alive. The coroner found that Jason's skull had been fractured. He also noted that Jason had over 28 fractures on various bones all over his body in various stages of healing. The coroner, John Meyer (the same one who autopsied JonBenet) pronounced it homicide. Naturally, Trip DeMuth said just because a ten-month-old has 28 broken bones doesn't mean it's murder. Well, despite Trip's best efforts to shield child-killers (again!) the police focused on little Jason's parents, Alex and Molly. Like the Ramseys, they hired lawyers and clammed up. And like the Ramseys, they had connections. DA Mary Lacy was reluctant to go forward, since Jason's grandfather, prominent Boulder architect J. Nold Midyette, owned half of the Pearl Street Mall. It took Mary Lacy being hounded in her own driveway by a news crew from Bill O'Reilly's television news analysis program, *The O'Reilly Factor*, to actually do anything about it. And even then, she turned it over to a grand jury. As it stands, Molly Midyette was given the minimum sentence of 16 years in prison for failing to help the baby after her husband beat him to death. In fancy legal terms, that's called "depraved indifference to human life." It's probably not a big surprise to anyone who has read this far in that she got off easy. Even then, she is eligible for parole in May 2014. Alex Midyette also was sentenced to 16 years in prison; he is serving his time at the Trinidad Correctional Facility and is eligible for parole in January 2016.. Like every two-bit hood since the beginning of time, he and his lawyers have hidden behind quirks in the law. And now it looks like Molly is about to turn on him as well. There truly is no honor among thieves.

Finally, we have the death of two-year-old Caylee Anthony, a Florida girl most likely killed by her mother, Casey Anthony. Casey, a stereotypical white-trash party girl, who didn't even know WHICH of her one-night stands was Caylee's father, was spotted partying in after-hours clubs after her daughter vanished, and did not report the girl missing for a month. Far as I'm concerned, that should have been it. Which arm do you want the needle in? Instead, after a legal battle that lasted three years, Casey was found not guilty and walked scot-free. She walked free, not because the prosecution didn't do a good job, but because, in this author's humble opinion, too many people who end up on juries are of substandard intelligence, unable to make common-sense judgments. And why is that? Because of the garbage the Ramseys and their supporters have fed us for years, about how modern technology is the end-all, be-all of investigation and circumstantial evidence is not "real" evidence. I wonder how many little children will have to die because of Ramsey propaganda. Well, I hold the Ramseys and their supporters responsible for every one of them.

The reason I mention these cases is because every now and then I can't help but wonder if, and it's a big if, people have figured they could kill their kids and get away with it because the Ramseys did, to their way of thinking. Other people have a different take on it: they see these people as victims of police conspiracies like the Ramseys claim they were.

Either way, justice has not been done.

CHAPTER FOURTEEN

Untruth, Injustice and the Un-American Way

A small-town boy from Vermont probably seems like an unlikely hero. Certainly, no one asked me to be JonBenet's knight in shining armor. But the way I see it, every little girl needs a hero. If not me, who? If you witness an injustice in your life, you can't and shouldn't be expected to wait for an engraved invitation. Somebody has to speak up, and while I can sympathize with the people who say, "don't get involved; it's not your fight," in the end it is a fight for the soul of humanity, and we'd damn well better fight it. As the old saying goes, all it takes for evil to triumph is for good men to do nothing. That's how I was raised. My parents may not have had the kind of wherewithal the Ramseys had, but they knew right from wrong and did the best they could to teach their sons.

I don't expect a lot of praise. I'm not out for glory. I'm just damn sick of this game where evil gains a foothold because the people we trust to protect us are weak, where the rich are afforded privileges that none of us who have to sweat to earn bread for our families could ever get, where someone who takes the life of another can buy their way free.

At the heart of this matter lies a little girl who is dead; a beautiful, innocent, precious angel who never did anything bad to anyone. If anyone deserved justice, JonBenet does. She deserves it more than anything. I believed that when I supported her parents, and I believe it now. This little girl was killed twice. First she was killed physically, and then her memory was defiled by deceit. The only thing more horrifying than the idea that a little child, one with everything going for her isn't safe in her own home is the idea that her killer was someone she loved. It rocks the comfort zone to think that it's not just the bums on Skid Row who could do something like this. It crosses all lines: race, class, gender, creed, nationality, age, seasons of the year, and time of day. The worst thing we can do is close our eyes, plug our ears and hold our tongues to reality. The sooner we face it, the sooner we can work to stop it.

It's too late for JonBenet. But it's not too late for all those other children out there. That should be JonBenet's legacy: she died, but others will live if her death tunes us in to the reality. If we can accomplish that, she will not have died for nothing. Hers would not be a wasted life.

On August 6th, 2008, JonBenet would have been eighteen-years-old. All grown up, she would have been looking forward to graduating high school. After that, who knows? She would have been great at anything she chose to do. She would also have been stunningly beautiful. The boys would be tripping over themselves to get close to her. Everything would be going her way. Imagine her family on prom night seeing her in her dress. Imagine the pride on the face of her date. And with luck, she would have had her own family in time. None of that will ever happen.

This case hurts. It hurts me every day. Not only because it happened, but because the person most likely responsible got away with it and was allowed to get away with it because nobody gave a damn. Taxpayer money was wasted, lives ruined, faith shattered, and none of it made any difference because the deck is stacked in the favor of killers.

When I was young, we said the Pledge of Allegiance every day at school. I was raised by my parents to believe in what the Pledge espouses. But as I get older, I realize that "And Justice For All" is nothing but a crock. And it's a crock because too many of us accept the insults done to it and to us. It's time we started to live up to our promises. Since JonBenet's parents can't be bothered to think about anyone but themselves, it's up to me. And you can do your part.

The current governor of Colorado is John Wright Hickenlooper, Jr. (born February 7, 1952), an American politician who has been Governor of Colorado since 2011. His office can appoint a special prosecutor to this case.

If you would like to help, you can sign an on-line petition to have a special prosecutor appointed. Just go to http://www.petitiononline.com/jbr246/ and sign up.

Pray for rain on this case, folks. In 2009, a new DA took office. His name is Stanley Garnett. Since he wasn't one of the original morons, there's some hope for him. But what good will it do?

EPILOGUE

Little Broken Doll

JonBenet Ramsey was exploited from the day she was born. She never had a chance. She was used to fulfill the needs of others, including needs best left in the darkness where they come from. After she died, she was exploited again, and for much the same reasons. Several words come to mind, including shameful, disgusting, revolting, and sick. None of them seem adequate to describe it.

She was a project for her mother and grandmother. The way I look at it, Grandma was upset that none of her daughters made it, so JonBenet was the next in line. Earlier in the book, I showed a picture of Patsy gripping JonBenet's arm. Here it is again:

Take another look, but not at the arm. Look at their faces. The smiles are very phony. No crinkles around the eyes. It's a "look-happy-for-the-camera smile." Patsy's cheeks look a little puffy, as though she'd been crying. The only redeeming quality about it is it shows how beautiful JonBenet was naturally, without a lot of makeup. It also shows what a naturally pretty woman Patsy was. They lived in a looks-are-everything world. Two wind-up dolls used for other people's pleasure. JonBenet's "Vegas" outfit is the same outfit her mom wore twenty years earlier. The cycle continues.

When JonBenet was killed, her exploiters realized that she could be worth more to them dead than she was alive. That's not an original idea. Like I said at the beginning, history is full of instances where people have been worth more to a cause or movement dead than they were alive, even if they didn't particularly subscribe to that cause.. The day of JonBenet's funeral, Patsy was concerned with how she looked. John told her she looked like Jackie O at JFK's funeral. That's appropriate when you consider how much the Ramseys have tried to emulate the Kennedys: a wealthy family with tragedy in their background; witness the mythology of John F. Kennedy, ruler of a Camelot presidency, struck down in the prime of life by unreasoning hatred because he dared to stand up for the little guy, despite his own privileged upbringing, leaving a young wife and little children to pick up the pieces.. It's largely a fabrication, but it's a nice story, so people believe it, just like they would rather believe a cockamamie story about a bogeyman intruder than think that a beautiful mother with money and an education could kill her daughter. We would all much rather believe that it's only the skanky people, the trailer-park dwellers, the ghetto denizens, who do that kind of thing. Both Ramseys have devoted considerable time and airspace trying to convince us of exactly that. John Ramsey has claimed that when a parent kills a child, there's always a long history of abuse and everyone knows about it. Again, that's a nice story, but common sense tells us that if it were the case, there wouldn't be so many dead children at the hands of their parents. That is a trap that far too many people fall into. We, as human beings, have a psychological need for killers, especially child killers, to be different from us, because it's just makes us too uncomfortable to realize that they are regular people like us. We want them to be obvious monsters—some drooling, leg-dragging hunchback, much like the king in Shakespeare's *Richard III*. The truth is, child-murders are committed by people who are outwardly very normal-seeming. Darlie Routier had no history of any kind before she murdered her two boys. Susan Smith had not been abusive to her boys before she murdered them. Diane Downs had not been abusive to her children before she killed them, neither had Marilyn Lemak or Casey Anthony. That's the problem with psychopaths: they don't always look like Charles Manson. They aren't all so easy to spot. It's a hard lesson for a cruel world, but we all had damn well better learn it: evil wears many masks. The mask of good is the most dangerous mask of all. One of the people who weighed in on this case early on was an incredibly courageous woman named Marilyn Van Derbur, herself a former Miss America and Denver resident. In her book, *Miss America By Day*, she tells the story of her own prominent Denver family, including her father, a pillar of the community who erected the famous giant cross that overlooks the city. Turned out he was a pervert who molested Marilyn and her sisters regularly, while her mother turned a blind eye to it. When her mother found out, she blamed

Marilyn. Marilyn's story has very effectively disabused me of my notions about who is and isn't a "good fit."

By contrast, the parents of Danielle Van Dam seem to fit that "profile" in many ways. They did drugs, they embraced the "swinger" lifestyle, and they were irresponsible in some ways. Yet they were never considered serious suspects by the authorities. I hope I'm not portraying them in a negative light, because they are incredibly brave, strong people who have suffered an unimaginable loss. They also hid nothing from the police and put their daughter ahead of petty concerns and useless grudges. Oh, and the actual killer, David Westerfield? No violent history.

For all of their protestations about having been crucified in the media, the Ramseys have themselves to blame for a considerable amount of it. They made the choice to hide behind lawyers rather than talk to the cops and tell all they knew when their memories were still fresh. They could have done that instead of making a whole mess of demands (which the DA was stupid enough to grant) and waiting until the only answers they could give were "I don't remember" and "I can't recall." Even Lou Smit said that if he had been on the case the first day he would have split them up and had them arrested if they didn't tell all they knew. Money, bureaucratic incompetence and gutlessness kept very likely child killers out of prison. The authorities in Boulder have no problem putting indigent black and Hispanic perps in prison for minor offenses, but weren't too keen on going after a former Miss West Virginia with a rich, well-connected husband whose law firm controlled half the state. This case should have been so easy to solve. It is easy to solve. It became difficult when a wealthy executive decided to use his wealth and connections to thwart justice.

The stink of the OJ Simpson trial hangs over this case like the sword of Damocles, both in the way that money was able to buy justice and how it was pursued. Think about it: the Los Angeles DA's office was a competent, experienced institution with a history of handling high-profile cases. In short, they were everything the Boulder DA's office wasn't. They had everything except the proverbial busload of nuns as eyewitnesses in that case and Simpson walked. What kind of message do you think that sent to a two-bit operation like the Boulder DA's office? I think it scared the shit out of them. There is more evidence against the Ramseys than there was against Scott Peterson, and he's on Death Row. He had no violent history either. But the Ramseys had one thing going for them that Scotty didn't: each other. That's the big reason why they never went to prison: because there was never enough evidence to charge one with the actual killing and the other with cover-up charges. As Schiller phrased it in *Perfect Murder, Perfect Town*, two suspects equals no suspects. It's a simple legal fact, which everyone from Alex Hunter to Wendy Murphy to Vincent Bugliosi agrees on: you can't charge two people with the same crime. You have to charge one with the killing and one with the cover-up. As Bugliosi himself said, quote:

"If we come to the conclusion that JonBenet was not murdered by an intruder, the inevitable question presents itself: which parent did it? A prosecutor can't argue to a jury, 'Ladies and gentlemen, the evidence is very clear here that either Mr. or Mrs. Ramsey committed this murder and the other one covered it up...' There is no case to take to the jury unless the DA could prove beyond a reasonable doubt which one of them did it." Bugliosi also echoed Pete Hofstrom by saying, "Even if you could prove beyond a reasonable doubt that Patsy Ramsey wrote the ransom note, that doesn't mean she committed the murder."

In her book, *And Justice For Some,* Murphy calls this the "cross-finger pointing defense." She elaborates by saying, quote:

"If police believe John killed JonBenet, Patsy's seeming involvement in aspects of the crime would frustrate prosecution efforts because of the very real risk that John could prevail at trial by pointing the finger at Patsy.

"Even if the prosecutors felt confident about the evidence, they had to worry about what jurors would think–and as an ethical matter, they couldn't proceed unless they believed they could persuade a jury about one parent's guilt beyond a reasonable doubt."

The Boulder authorities were dealt a bad hand in another way: under Colorado law, no lesser charges could have been filed as long as the murder charge hadn't been filed, which meant that lesser offenses like obstruction of justice, making false statements and tampering with evidence, which could have easily been brought in this case, were not an option.

I always tell people not to blame the police because you can't enforce laws that don't exist. In an article for the conservative periodical, *National Review,* dated one week before the September 11th attacks, author William Tucker reminds us that two-bit hoods have always been able to hide behind some quirk in the law and that the courts have made it easier for them to do so, thanks to the rulings of judges with Alex Hunter's political leanings. Whether you agree with the magazine's political position or not, I think we can all agree that all of us (or at least the great majority of us) have a common interest in seeing crimes solved.

Another problem is that nobody can seem to unglue the DA's lips off of John Ramsey's ass.

Sometimes I wonder what would have happened if the Ramseys had gone to trial. I always come out the same way: a plea bargain, quick, efficient and out the door, just the way the Boulder DA likes it. Whether the Ramseys asked for one or not, it wouldn't matter, since the result would be the same. The Ramseys would spend very little prison time, if any at all. But whatever way you slice it, they would have to live with it. Maybe that's the key to this mess: the authorities in Boulder, so opposed to the death penalty, probably couldn't stomach the idea of putting a beautiful mother who just lost her daughter and was obviously very distraught about it in prison for the rest of her life, even death row. Even a short prison sentence would most likely have proven fatal to a woman in fragile health. Maybe she suffered enough. As Shakespeare said so eloquently, "the quality of mercy is not strained. It blesseth he who gives and he who takes."

Then again, it's been speculated that the Ramseys would have fled the country if indictments came down. They could have hung around with Roman Polanski, I guess.

The one thing I find sleazy about this whole thing is the "God" angle. I've always wondered how the Ramseys could live with themselves if they did this horrible crime. I only come out with two options: they figured they had to save their remaining child, or they chalked it up to "God's will," or some other damn thing. After all, they were a very religious family, as I mentioned, and they used that religiousness to try and prove their innocence. They said that JonBenet had fulfilled her purpose in life; that was all God had laid out for her. Isn't that convenient? Hey, their revival tent show fooled Lou Smit, why not the rest of us? They always asked how two God-fearing people could commit such a crime. I think it's damn sleazy to hide behind religion instead of presenting hard evidence of innocence. From what I've presented, hard evidence didn't exist.

This case was a tragedy right across the board. Let me be clear on one thing: even if I had good reason, I don't hate Patsy Ramsey. At one time, I may have, but hate's not worth wasting your life on, so I gave it up. And I have never doubted that Patsy Ramsey loved her daughter with everything in her being. I have never doubted that. Patsy Ramsey was a loving mother and an amazing wife and a great friend to everyone who knew her. She was a gorgeous, smart, dynamic lady. In my heart I know she didn't mean for any of this to happen. Even after my "conversion," I always wanted to protect her, to hug her and say, "it will be all right. Just tell the truth and it will be all right. I promise." I do not blame her for this. Her mother distorted her mind so badly from such a young age she didn't know any better. Her marriage didn't help. And only the gods know what kind of damage her treatments and drugs did to her mind. This is an area I believe must be researched more fully. If these drugs have these dangerous side effects, we owe it to JonBenet and we owe it to Patsy to make sure that nothing like this happens again.

When I heard that Patsy had died, I was shattered. I didn't leave my house for two days. I mourned her passing for a long time. If I had been with her, I would have told her, "Patsy, it's all right. Don't be afraid. I forgive you. JonBenet forgives you. She doesn't hate you, she loves you. She will always love you. And she needs her mommy. The gods have forgiven you. They will show mercy. Don't be afraid of death." And letting her pass, I can see her in the next world, a world of sunshine and joy, having escaped the torment of hell. The hell she suffered on Earth is enough. She can see her beautiful little daughter running to see her, to embrace her again.

"Mommy!"

"I'm here, baby!"

They are together again now, dancing with the gods, all pain forgotten, with only love between them. A mother and daughter are together again, never to be parted, just as it should be. May they find eternal happiness. I know there are people who will disagree with me, thinking she does not deserve forgiveness, but I like to think that. It gives me hope for myself and the rest of us to think that.

I also extend my sincerest sympathies to Burke Ramsey. I can't even imagine what these last two decades have been like for him. I also know what it means to lose a mother to cancer. It's the worst thing in the world.

This is how I'll always remember JonBenet: a Christmas angel, surrounded by winter, forever young, forever beautiful. I know I should be angry, but I'm not. I may have forgiven Patsy Ramsey, but no one else. Absolutely not. That's why I'm not angry: because, as the Sicilians say, revenge is a dish best served cold. I'm coming, and hell is coming with me.

APPENDIX A

Steve Thomas's Resignation Letter
August 6, 1998

Chief Beckner,

On June 22, I submitted a letter to Chief Koby, requesting a leave of absence from the Boulder Police Department. In response to persistent speculation as to why I chose to leave the Ramsey investigation, this letter explains more fully those reasons. Although my concerns were well known for some time, I tried to be gracious in my departure, addressing only health concerns. However, after a month of soul searching and reflection, I feel I must now set the record straight.

The primary reason I chose to leave is my belief that the district attorney's office continues to mishandle the Ramsey case. I had been troubled for many months with many aspects of the investigation. Albeit an uphill battle of a case to begin with, it became a nearly impossible investigation because of the political alliances, philosophical differences, and professional egos that blocked progress in more ways, and on more occasions, than I can detail in this memorandum. I and others voiced these concerns repeatedly. In the interest of hoping justice would be served, we tolerated it, except for those closed door sessions when detectives protested in frustration, where fists hit the table, where detectives demanded that the right things be done. The wrong things were done, and made it a manner of simple principle that I could not continue to participate as it stood with the district attorney's office. As an organization, we remained silent, when we should have shouted.

The Boulder Police Department took a handful of detectives days after the murder, and handed us this case. As one of those five primary detectives, we tackled it for a year and a half. We conducted an exhaustive investigation, followed the evidence where it led us, and were faithfully and professionally committed to this case. Although not perfect, cases rarely are. During eighteen months on the Ramsey investigation, my colleagues and I worked the case night and day, and in spite of tied hands. On June 1-2, 1998, we crunched thirty thousand pages of investigation to its essence, and put our cards on the table, delivering the case in a formal presentation to the district attorney's office. We stood confident in our work. Very shortly thereafter, though, the detectives who know this case better than anyone were advised by the district attorney's office that we would not be participating as grand jury advisory witnesses.

The very entity with whom we shared our investigative case file to see justice sought, I felt, was betraying this case. We were never afforded true prosecutorial support. There was never a consolidation of resources. All legal opportunities were not made available. How were we expected to "solve" this case when the district attorney's office was crippling us with their positions? I believe they were, literally, facilitating the escape of justice. During this investigation, consider the following:

During the investigation detectives would discover, collect, and bring evidence to the district attorney's office, only to have it summarily dismissed or rationalized as insignificant. The most elementary of investigative efforts, such as obtaining telephone and credit card records, were met without support, search warrants denied. The significant opinions of national experts were casually dismissed or ignored by the district attorney's office, even the experienced FBI were waved aside.

Those who chose not to cooperate were never compelled before a grand jury early in this case, as detectives suggested only weeks after the murder, while information and memories were fresh.

An informant, for reasons his own, came to detectives about conduct occurring inside the district attorney's office, including allegations of a plan intended only to destroy a man's career. We carefully listened. With that knowledge, the department did nothing. Other than to alert the accused, and in the process burn the two detectives [who captured that exchange on an undercover wire, incidentally] who came forth with this information. One of the results of that internal whistleblowing was witnessing Detective Commander Eller, who also could not tolerate what was occurring, lose his career and reputation undeservedly; scapegoated in a manner which only heightened my concerns. It did not take much inferential reasoning to realize that any dissidents were readily silenced.

In a departure from protocol, police reports, physical evidence, and investigative information was shared with Ramsey defense attorneys, all of this in the district attorney's office "spirit of cooperation". I served a search warrant, only to find later defense attorneys were simply given copies of the evidence it yielded.

An FBI agent, whom I didn't even know, quietly tipped me off about what the DA's office was doing behind our backs, conducting investigation the police department was wholly unaware of.

I was advised not to speak to certain witnesses, and all but dissuaded from pursuing particular investigative efforts. Polygraphs were acceptable for some subjects, but others seemed immune from such requests.

Innocent people were not "cleared", publicly or otherwise, even when it was unmistakably the right thing to do, as reputations and lives were destroyed.

Some in the district attorney's office, to this day, pursue weak, defenseless, and innocent people in shameless tactics that one couldn't believe more bizarre if it were made up.

I was told by one in the district attorney's office about being unable to "break" a particular police officer from his resolute accounts of events he had witnessed. In my opinion, this was not trial preparation, this was an attempt to derail months of hard work.

I was repeatedly reminded by some in the district attorney's office just how powerful and talented and resourceful particular defense attorneys were. How could decisions be made this way?

There is evidence that was critical to the investigation, that to this day has never been collected, because neither search warrants nor other means were supported to do so. Not to mention evidence which still sits today, untested in the laboratory, as differences continue about how to proceed.

While investigative efforts were rebuffed, my search warrant affidavits and attempts to gather evidence in the murder investigation of a six year old child were met with refusals and, instead, the suggestion that we "ask the permission of the Ramseys" before proceeding. And just before conducting the Ramsey interviews, I thought it inconceivable I was being lectured on "building trust".

These are but a few of the many examples of why I chose to leave. Having to convince, to plead at times, to a district attorney's office to assist us in the murder of a little girl, by way of the most basic of investigative requests, was simply absurd.

When my detective partner and I had to literally hand search tens of thousands of receipts, because we didn't have a search warrant to assist us otherwise, we did so. But we lost tremendous opportunities to make progress, to seek justice, and to know the truth. Auspicious timing and strategy could have made a difference. When the might of the criminal justice system should have brought all it had to bear on this investigation, and didn't, we remained silent. We were trying to deliver a murder case with hands tied behind our backs. It was difficult, and our frustrations understandable. It was an assignment without chance of success. Politics seemed to trump justice.

Even "outsiders" quickly assessed the situation, as the FBI politely noted early on: "the government isn't in charge of this investigation." As the nation watched, appropriately anticipating a fitting response to the murder of the most innocent of victims, I stood bothered as to what occurred behind the scenes. Those inside this case knew what was going on. Eighteen months gave us a unique perspective.

We learned to ignore the campaign of misinformation in which we were said to be bumbling along, or else just pursuing one or two suspects in some ruthless vendetta. Much of what appeared in the press was orchestrated by particular sources wishing to discredit the Boulder Police Department. We watched the media spun, while we were prohibited from exercising First Amendment rights. As disappointment and frustration pervaded, detectives would remark to one another, "if it reaches a particular point, I'm walking away."

But we would always tolerate it "just one more time." Last year, when we discovered hidden cameras inside the Ramsey house, only to realize the detectives had been unwittingly videotaped, this should have rocked the police department off its foundation. Instead, we allowed that, too, to pass without challenge.

The detectives' enthusiasm became simply resigned frustration, acquiescing to that which should never have been tolerated. In the media blitz, the pressure of the whole world watching, important decisions seemed to be premised on "how it would play" publicly.

Among at least a few of the detectives, "there's something wrong here" became a catch phrase. I witnessed others having to make decisions which impacted their lives and careers, watched the soul searching that occurred as the ultimate questions were pondered. As it goes, "evils that befall the world are not nearly so often caused by bad men, as they are by good men who are silent when an opinion must be voiced." Although several good men in the police department shouted loudly behind closed doors, the organization stood deafeningly silent at what continued to occur unchallenged.

Last Spring, you, too, seemed at a loss. I was taken aback when I was reminded of what happened to Commander Eller when he stuck his neck out. When reminded how politically powerful the DA was. When reminded of the hundreds of other cases the department had to file with this district attorney's office, and that this was but one case. And finally, when I was asked, "what do you want done? The system burned down?", it struck me dumb. But when you conceded that there were those inside the DA's office we had to simply accept as "defense witnesses", and when we were reduced to simply recording our objections for "documentation purposes" —I knew I was not going to participate in this much longer.

I believe the district attorney's office is thoroughly compromised. When we were told by one in the district attorney's office, months before we had even completed our investigation, that this case "is not prosecutable," we shook our heads in disbelief. A lot could have been forgiven, the lesser transgressions ignored, for the right things done. Instead, those in the district attorney's office encouraged us to allow them to "work their magic" (which I never fully understood. Did that "magic" include sharing our case file information with the defense attorneys, dragging feet in evidence collection, or believing that two decades of used-car-dealing-style-plea-bargaining was somehow going to solve this case?). Right and wrong is just that. Some of these issues were not shades of gray. Decision should have been made as such. Whether a suspect a penniless indigent with a public defender, or otherwise.

As contrasted by my experiences in Georgia, for example, where my warrant affidavits were met with a sense of support and an obligation to the victim. Having worked with able prosecutors in other jurisdictions, having worked cases where justice was aggressively sought, I have familiarity with these prosecution professionals who hold a strong sense of justice. And then, from Georgia, the Great Lakes, the East Coast, the South, I would return to Boulder, to again be thoroughly demoralized.

We delayed and ignored, for far too long, that which was "right", in deference of maintaining this dysfunctional relationship with the district attorney's office. This wasn't a runaway train that couldn't be stopped. Some of us bit our tongues as the public was told of this "renewed cooperation" between the police department and the district attorney's office —this at the very time the detectives and those in the district attorney's office weren't even on speaking terms, the same time you had to act as a liaison between the two agencies because the detectives couldn't tolerate it. I was quite frankly surprised, as you remarked on this camaraderie, that there had not yet been a fistfight.

In Boulder, where the politics, policies, and pervasive thought has held for years, a criminal justice system designed to deal with such an event was not in place. Instead, we had an institution that when needed most, buckled. The system was paralyzed, as to this day one continues to get away with murder.

Will there be a real attempt at justice? I may be among the last to find out. The department assigned me some of the most sensitive and critical assignments in the Ramsey case, including search warrants and affidavits, the Atlanta projects, the interviews of the Ramseys, and many other sensitive assignments I won't mention. I criss-crossed the country, conducting interviews and investigation, pursuing pedophiles and drifters, chasing and discarding leads. I submitted over 250 investigative reports for this case alone. I'd have been happy to assist the grand jury. But the detectives, who know this case better than anyone, were told we would not be allowed as grand jury advisory witnesses, as is common place. If a grand jury is convened, the records will be sealed, and we will not witness what goes on inside such a proceeding.

What part of the case gets presented, what doesn't?

District Attorney Hunter's continued reference to a "runaway" grand jury is also puzzling. Is he afraid that he cannot control the outcome? Why would one not simply present evidence to jurors, and let the jury decide?

Perhaps the DA is hoping for a voluntary confession one day. What's needed, though, is an effective district attorney to conduct the inquiry, not a remorseful killer.

The district attorney's office should be the ethical and judicial compass for the community, ensuring that justice is served —or at least, sought. Instead, our DA has becoming a spinning compass for the media. The perpetuating inference continues that justice is somehow just around the corner. I do not see that occurring, as the two year anniversary of this murder approaches.

It is my belief the district attorney's office has effectively crippled this case. The time for intervention is now. It is difficult to imagine a more compelling situation for the appointment of an entirely independent prosecution team to be introduced into this matter, who would oversee an attempt at righting this case.

* * * * *

Unmistakably and worst of all, we have failed a little girl named Jon Benet. Six years old. Many good people, decent, innocent citizens, are forever bound by the murder of this child. There is a tremendous obligation to them. But an infinitely greater obligation to her, as she rests in a small cemetery far away from this anomaly of a place called Boulder.

A distant second stands the second tragedy —the failure of the system in Boulder. Ask the mistreated prosecution witnesses in this investigation, who cooperated for months, who now refuse to talk until a special prosecutor is established. Ask former detectives who have quietly tendered their shields in disheartenment. Ask all those innocent people personally affected by this case, who have had their lives upset because of the arbitrary label of "suspect" being attached. Ask the cops who cannot speak out because they still wear a badge. The list is long.

I know that to speak out brings its own issues. But as you also know, there are others who are as disheartened as I am, who are biting their tongues, searching their consciences. I know what may occur —I may be portrayed as frustrated, disgruntled. Not so.

I have had an exemplary and decorated thirteen year career as a police officer and detective.

I didn't want to challenge the system. In no way do I wish to harm this case or subvert the long and arduous work that has been done. I only wish to speak up and ask for assistance in making a change. I want justice for a child who was killed in her home on Christmas night.

This case has defined many aspects of all our lives, and will continue to do so for all of our days. My colleagues put their hearts and souls into this case, and I will take some satisfaction that it was the detective team who showed tremendous efforts and loyalties to seeking justice for this victim. Many sacrifices were made. Families. Marriages. In the latter months of the investigation, I was diagnosed with a disease which will require a lifetime of medication.

Although my health declined, I was resolved to see the case through to a satisfactory closure. I did that on June 1-2. And on June 22, I requested a leave of absence, without mention of what transpired in our department since Christmas 1996.

What I witnessed for two years of my life was so fundamentally flawed, it reduced me to tears. Everything the badge ever meant to me was so foundationally shaken, one should never have to sell one's soul as a prerequisite to wear it. On June 26, after leaving the investigation for the last time, and leaving the city of Boulder, I wept as I drove home, removing my detectives shield and placing it on the seat beside me, later putting it in a desk drawer at home, knowing I could never put it back on.

There is some consolation that a greater justice awaits the person who committed these acts, independent of this system we call "justice." A greater justice awaits. Of that, at least, we can be confident.

As a now infamous author, panicked in the night, once penned, "use that good southern common sense of yours." I will do just that.

Originally from a small southern town where this would never have been tolerated, where respect for law and order and traditions were instilled in me, I will take that murderous author's out-of-context advice. And use my good southern common sense to put this case into the perspective it necessitates —a precious child was murdered. There needs to be some consequence to that.

Regretfully, I tender this letter, and my police career, a calling which I loved. I do this because I cannot continue to sanction by my silence what has occurred in this case. It was never a fair playing field, the "game" was simply unacceptable anymore. And that's what makes this all so painful. The detectives never had a chance. If ever there were a case, and if ever there were a victim, who truly meant something to the detectives pursuing the truth, this is it. If not this case, what case? Until such time an independent prosecutor is appointed to oversee this case, I will not be a part of this. What went on was simply wrong.

I recalled a favorite passage recently, Atticus Finch speaking to his daughter: "Just remember that one thing does not abide by majority rule, Scout —it's your conscience."

At thirty-six years old, I thought my life's passion as a police officer was carved in stone. I realize that although I may have to trade my badge for a carpenter's hammer, I will do so with a clear conscience. It is with a heavy heart that I offer my resignation from the Boulder Police Department, in protest of this continuing travesty.

[Signed]
Detective Steve Thomas #638
Detective Division
Boulder Police Department
August 6, 1998

BIBLIOGRAPHY

Bardach 1997. Anne Louise Bardach. "Who Killed JonBenet?" *Vanity Fair, September 16, 1997.* Full article can be accessed at: http://thewebsafe.tripod.com/09161997 vanityfair.htm

Brennan 2003. Charlie Brennan. U.S. judge's Ramsey ruling questioned. *Rocky Mountain News, April 24, 2003*

Carnes 2003. Federal District Court Judge Julie Carnes Opinion in Wolf v. Ramsey, March 31, 2003

Foster 2000. Donald Foster. *Author Unknown: On the Trail of Anonymous (Hardcover). Henry Holt & Company, November 2000*

Kolar 2012 A James Kolar. *Foreign Faction–Who Really Kidnapped JonBenet? Ventus Publishing, llc (June 14, 2012)*

Lakin 2005. Peggy Lakin. *Journey Beyond Reason. Ebookstand. com (E-book).* www.peggy-lakin.com.

Maloney & O'Connor 2003. J.J. Maloney and J. Patrick O'Connor. The Murder of JonBenét Ramsey. *Crime Magazine. May 7, 1999, updated 2/20/01, 4/20/03, 8/30/06 and 7/20/08*

Miller, 2001. Thomas Miller, Salute to American Justice: Colorado v. Miller 99 CR 2023. Pearl Street Press, LLC. (CD-ROM)

Ramsey & Ramsey 2000. John and Patsy Ramsey. *Death of Innocence: The Untold Story of JonBenét's Murder and How*

Its Exploitation Compromised the Pursuit of Truth (Hardcover). Nelson Books, 2000.

Ross 2003. Ryan Ross. Solving the JonBenét Case, *Crime Magazine, April 14, 2003.*

Schiller 1999. Lawrence Schiller. *Perfect Murder, Perfect Town : The Uncensored Story of the JonBenet Murder and the Grand Jury's Search for the Final Truth (Paperback). HarperTorch, November 1999.*

Thomas 2000. Steve Thomas with Donald A. Davis. *JonBenét (Paperback). St. Martin's Paperbacks, November 15, 2000.*

Wecht & Bosworth 1998. Wecht, Cyril H. and Charles Bosworth, Jr. *Who Killed JonBenét? A Leading Forensic Expert Uncovers the Shocking Facts (Paperback). Onyx Books, July 1998.*

http://www.jonbenetindexguide.com/1997BPD-Patsy-Interview-Complete.htm

http://www.jonbenetindexguide.com/1997BPD-John-Interview-Complete.htm

http://www.jonbenetindexguide.com/1998BPD-Patsy-Interview-Complete.htm

http://www.jonbenetindexguide.com/2000ATL-Patsy-Interview-Complete.htm

http://www.jonbenetindexguide.com/2000ATL-John-Interview-Complete.htm

http://www.jonbenetindexguide.com/09212001Depo-SteveThomas.htm

http://www.jonbenetindexguide.com/11262001Depo-MarkBeckner.htm

http://jonbenetindexguide.com/12112001Depo-PatsyRamsey.htm

http://www.jonbenetindexguide.com/12122001Depo-JohnRamsey.htm

http://www.jonbenetindexguide.com/05132002Depo-CinaWong.htm

http://www.jonbenetindexguide.com/05172002Depo-GideonEpstein.htm

http://www.acandyrose.com/03312003carnes01-10.htm

http://www.dailycamera.com

http://www.denverpost.com

http://www.rockymountainnews.com